FOR SUCH A
TIME AS THIS

Ruth and Esther

NELSON
IMPACT™
Bible Study Series

FOR SUCH A
TIME AS THIS

Ruth and Esther

NELSON IMPACT
A Division of Thomas Nelson Publishers
Since 1798

www.thomasnelson.com

Published by Nelson Impact, a Division of Thomas Nelson, Inc., P.O. Box 141000, Nashville, Tennessee, 37214.

Scripture quotations marked NKJV are taken from the *The Holy Bible,* The New King James Version®. Copyright © 1979, 1980, 1982, Thomas Nelson, Inc., Publishers.

ISBN 1-4185-0617-6

Printed in the United States of America.

06 07 08 EB 9 8 7 6 5 4 3 2 1

A Word from the Publisher...

Be diligent to present yourself approved to God, a worker who does not need to be ashamed, rightly dividing the word of truth.

2 Timothy 2:15 NKJV

We are so glad that you have chosen this study guide to enrich your biblical knowledge and strengthen your walk with God. Inside you will find great information that will deepen your understanding and knowledge of this book of the Bible.

Many tools are included to aid you in your study, including ancient and present-day maps of the Middle East, as well as timelines and charts to help you understand when the book was written and why. You will also benefit from sidebars placed strategically throughout this study guide, designed to give you expanded knowledge of language, theology, culture, and other details regarding the Scripture being studied.

We consider it a joy and a ministry to serve you and teach you through these study guides. May your heart be blessed, your mind expanded, and your spirit lifted as you walk through God's Word.

Blessings,

Edward (Les) Middleton, M.Div.
Editor-in-Chief, Nelson Impact

Timeline of Old

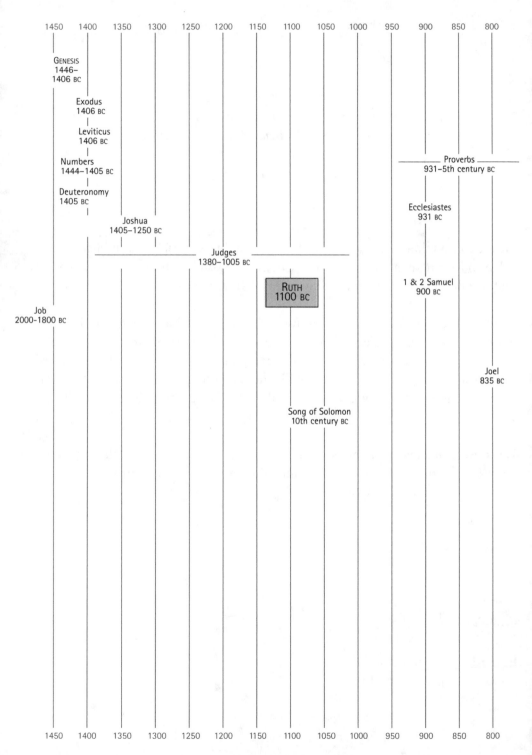

| 1450 | 1400 | 1350 | 1300 | 1250 | 1200 | 1150 | 1100 | 1050 | 1000 | 950 | 900 | 850 | 800 |

Genesis
1446–
1406 BC

Exodus
1406 BC

Leviticus
1406 BC

Numbers
1444–1405 BC

Deuteronomy
1405 BC

Joshua
1405–1250 BC

Judges
1380–1005 BC

Ruth
1100 BC

Job
2000–1800 BC

Proverbs
931–5th century BC

Ecclesiastes
931 BC

1 & 2 Samuel
900 BC

Joel
835 BC

Song of Solomon
10th century BC

| 1450 | 1400 | 1350 | 1300 | 1250 | 1200 | 1150 | 1100 | 1050 | 1000 | 950 | 900 | 850 | 800 |

TESTAMENT WRITINGS

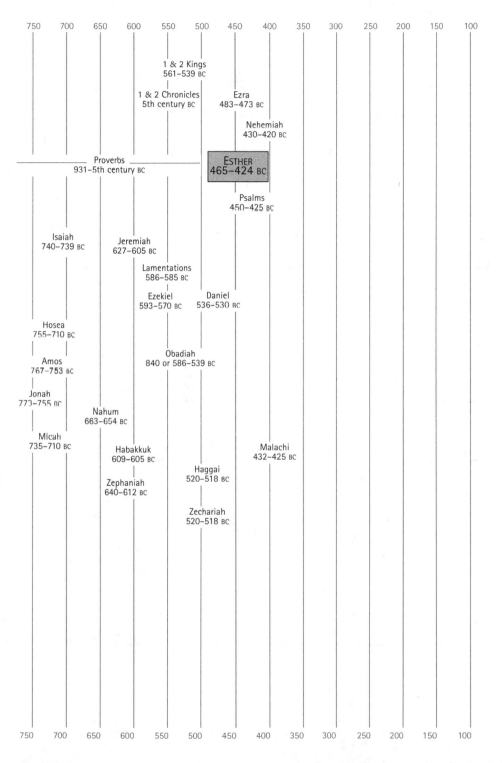

750   700   650   600   550   500   450   400   350   300   250   200   150   100

1 & 2 Kings
561–539 BC

1 & 2 Chronicles
5th century BC

Ezra
483–473 BC

Nehemiah
430–420 BC

Proverbs
931–5th century BC

ESTHER
465–424 BC

Psalms
450–425 BC

Isaiah
740–739 BC

Jeremiah
627–605 BC

Lamentations
586–585 BC

Ezekiel
593–570 BC

Daniel
536–530 BC

Hosea
755–710 BC

Obadiah
840 or 586–539 BC

Amos
767–753 BC

Jonah
773–755 BC

Nahum
663–654 BC

Micah
735–710 BC

Habakkuk
609–605 BC

Malachi
432–425 BC

Haggai
520–518 BC

Zephaniah
640–612 BC

Zechariah
520–518 BC

750   700   650   600   550   500   450   400   350   300   250   200   150   100

OLD MIDDLE EAST

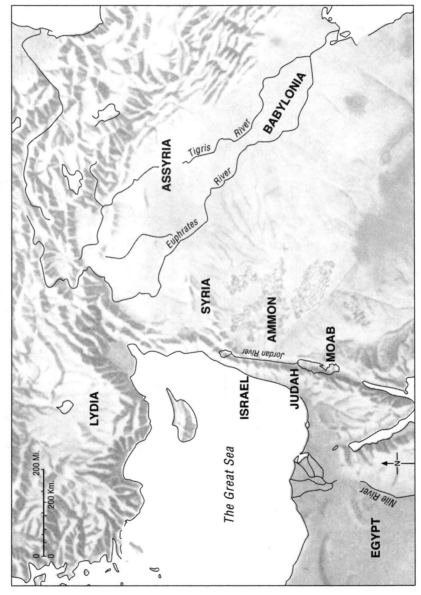

LYDIA

ASSYRIA

Tigris River

Euphrates River

BABYLONIA

SYRIA

AMMON

Jordan River

ISRAEL

JUDAH

MOAB

The Great Sea

Nile River

EGYPT

200 Mi.

200 Km.

N

MIDDLE EAST OF TODAY

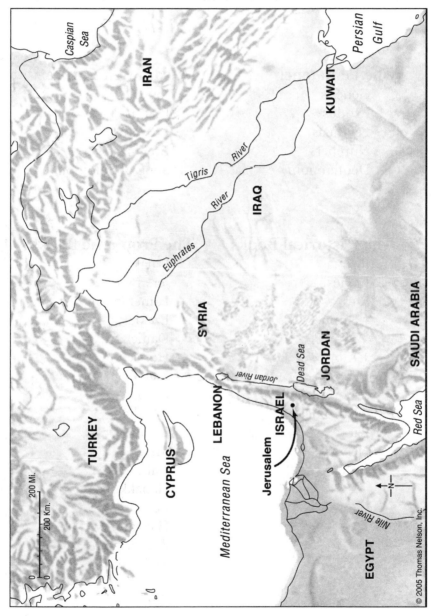

OLD TESTAMENT DIVISIONS

The Pentateuch
Genesis
Exodus
Leviticus
Numbers
Deuteronomy

Wisdom Literature
Job
Psalms
Proverbs
Ecclesiastes
Song of Solomon

The Historical Books
Joshua
Judges
Ruth
1 Samuel
2 Samuel
1 Kings
2 Kings
1 Chronicles
2 Chronicles
Ezra
Nehemiah
Esther

The Prophetic Books
Isaiah
Jeremiah
Lamentations
Ezekiel
Daniel
Hosea
Joel
Amos
Obadiah
Jonah
Micah
Nahum
Habakkuk
Zephaniah
Haggai
Zechariah
Malachi

New Testament Divisions

The Four Gospels
Matthew
Mark
Luke
John

History
Acts

The Epistles of Paul
Romans
1 Corinthians
2 Corinthians
Galatians
Ephesians
Philippians
Colossians
1 Thessalonians
2 Thessalonians
1 Timothy
2 Timothy
Titus
Philemon

The General Epistles
Hebrews
James
1 Peter
2 Peter
1 John
2 John
3 John
Jude

Apocalyptic Literature
Revelation

ICON KEY

Throughout this study guide, you will find many icon sidebars that will aid and enrich your study of this book of the Bible. To help you identify what these icons represent, please refer to the key below.

BIBLICAL GRAB BAG

A biblical grab bag full of interesting facts and tidbits.

BIBLE

Further exploration of biblical principles and interpretations, along with a little food for thought.

LANGUAGE

Word usages, definitions, interpretations, and information on the Greek and Hebrew languages.

CULTURE

Customs, traditions, and lifestyle practices in biblical times.

ARCHAEOLOGICAL

Archaeological discoveries and artifacts that relate to biblical life, as well as modern-day discoveries.

PREFACE

WHAT IS IT ABOUT RUTH AND ESTHER?

Why are the books of Ruth and Esther so often presented together in Bible handbooks and study guides of this type? I can think of several reasons. First, Ruth and Esther are the only two books in the Bible that are named for women, and that focus almost entirely on the stories of the women in the titles.

Second, both are relatively short (the books, not the women!), and though the messages they deliver are certainly profound and intensely meaningful, in theological terms they do not require huge volumes of explanation.

Both present uplifting stories that have functioned as positive role models for countless generations. Who has not marveled at the faithfulness of Ruth, the integrity of Boaz, the courage of Esther, or the wisdom of Mordecai?

Beyond all this, however, at least one other link connects the stories of these two women—and perhaps it's even more significant than anything mentioned above. Esther was a Jewish woman who married a Gentile man. Ruth was a gentile woman who married a Jewish man. Yet even though their situations were so different from one another, both were used by God.

Indeed, had it not been for Esther, a huge population of Jewish people would have been annihilated. The ultimate survival of the Jews might not have been threatened—for no one will *ever* succeed in killing them all—but certainly the world would have seen a serious reduction in their numbers, which easily could have carried over into the present day. And had it not been for Ruth, who literally became the great-grandmother of David, the very lineage of Christ would have been changed.

Of course, God is not limited by human circumstances. Surely He would have found some other way to protect His people and establish His Son's earthly ancestry. But that's not the point—He chose to accomplish both of these purposes through these two extraordinary women. One belonged to the nation of Israel by birth; the other was born a foreigner, found herself "grafted in" by marriage, and was then given a permanent inheritance in God's kingdom by her own very real, honorable, uncompromising choice.

The latter would be Ruth, of course, so let us begin with her.

CONTENTS

RUTH

INTRODUCTION

The story of Ruth is one of the most familiar in the Bible. It is read by orthodox Jews every year at the Feast of Firstfruits to commemorate the beginning of the harvest season. But it's also a strong favorite among non-Jews as well.

Ruth's famous "Entreat me not to leave you" speech has been repeated thousands and thousands of times in songs, book titles, speeches, and even wedding vows. Ironically, Ruth addressed those famous words to her mother-in-law. Logically, the love between Ruth and Boaz—not Ruth and Naomi—is what we might expect to be celebrated during a marriage ceremony.

But never mind. The simple fact is that the story of Ruth contains several brilliant examples of pure, unadulterated love, respect, and honor.

God loved Ruth enough to guarantee her safety among the Israelites, even though she came from the land of Moab. He also made her the great-grandmother of David, which put her in the middle of the line of ancestry leading directly to His own Son.

Ruth loved Naomi enough to leave the comparative security of her own country, her own relatives, and all the friends we can presume she must have had among her own people. She gave all that up to go with her widowed mother-in-law back to the land of Naomi's birth so that Naomi (but not necessarily Ruth) could find her own security among her own people.

Boaz loved God and honored God's established rules enough to see that Ruth obtained food both for herself and for Naomi. He also protected her from other men, from gossip, and eventually—even though he was quite a bit older—from the poverty and loneliness of old age without a husband and/or a son to care for her. Oh yes—Boaz loved her as well . . . but this was not what got the ball rolling!

Finally, of course, Ruth obviously trusted God and esteemed Boaz highly enough to deal honestly and respectfully with him as her kinsman redeemer. She could have attempted to seduce him, as Tamar did with her father-in-law, Judah (Gen. 38:11–30), when Judah failed to honor his own responsibilities many generations earlier (although the law Judah refused to observe was not the kinsman redeemer law—see "Levirate Marriage and Kinsman Redemption—Which Is Which?" in chapter 4 of this study guide).

But Ruth apparently realized that anything gained by feminine wiles could never be as satisfying as what came to her by honoring the laws, the customs, and most of all the God of her new people.

Small wonder, then, that the book of Ruth also serves as an object lesson on several levels at once.

THE AUTHOR AND THE BACKGROUND

Authorship of the books of Samuel and Judges is generally assigned to Samuel. Most scholars agree with Jewish tradition that Samuel also wrote Ruth, although we have very little internal proof. If they are correct, he probably did so near the time of David's ascension to the crown as king of Israel. Thus God might have used Samuel to write Ruth's story to establish the legitimacy of David's kingship as well as the legitimacy of God's own Son.

Since Ruth was the great-grandmother of David, we know she must have lived sometime during the last half of the twelfth century BC. This might well have made her a contemporary of Gideon, the fifth in a series of twelve judges who replaced

Moses in the years between his death and the anointings of Saul and David, the first two Israelite kings.

The time of the judges is not considered a time of great faith among the children of Israel. On the contrary, in many ways it was a dark age, a time of rudderless drifting, a time of apostasy, of repeatedly defying the God of Israel by doing precisely what He had long since warned His people against. Consider the actions of just three of those twelve leaders:

Gideon demonstrated tremendous faith in the face of overwhelming odds when he defeated the Midianites, the Amalekites, and the other desert tribes (Judg. 7:12, 17–21). But once his military service ended, Gideon began to leave God out of his life. Eventually he had many wives and concubines, with whom he produced seventy sons.

After Gideon died, one of his sons—**Abimelech**—killed all the others except one and thus established himself as a "king" on his own terms, godless and bloody though he might have been.

Samson is perhaps the best known of the judges, but generally not for good reasons. Samson was the ultimate example of a man to whom God gave overwhelming physical strength but who seemed to have almost no spiritual and moral character to counterbalance that one massive asset.

The book of Judges ends with these ominous words: "In those days there was no king in Israel; everyone did what was right in his own eyes" (Judg. 21:25 NKJV). For this reason alone, the story of Ruth stood in stark relief against a dark background of repeated idol worship, sexual debauchery, and other forms of licentiousness that characterized even the lives of Israel's leaders.

Yet in the middle of all this came a young woman from a country with an even darker past, who had more character, more personal honor, and more pure faith in the God of Israel than many of her new countrymen.

RESPONSIBILITY IN ACTION

If we had to use one word to sum up the main message of the book of Ruth, perhaps that word would be *responsibility*. For example, as the story of Ruth demonstrates, we know that God always honors His responsibilities to us. He always finds a way to carry out His plans for our welfare, whatever those plans might be.

We know too little about Elimelech, Naomi's husband, for him to be anything more than a minor player. However, we cannot credit him with acting too responsibly, given his inclination to leave Israel and migrate to Moab when things got tough.

On the other hand, his wife, Naomi, acted responsibly by returning to the sacred land of her birth as soon as the male members of her family had all passed away, thus freeing her from her obligation to stay with them wherever they went.

Orpah, Ruth's sister-in-law, acted on her own feelings by returning to her native Moab and her Moabite gods. It's hard to judge her harshly, yet perhaps it's fair to say that she essentially rejected the God of Israel by the choice she made, even though returning to her homeland was obviously the "safe" thing to do from a worldly perspective.

Ruth and Boaz, of course, both epitomized responsible conduct. Ruth stayed with Naomi out of the purest kind of love, to protect and care for her. She also stayed with the one true God, rejecting all the temptations of her upbringing in His favor.

Boaz did exactly as Israelite law and custom required, as dictated by God Himself. He was not necessarily in love with

Ruth, although love certainly came later. But he had the utmost respect both for her and for the God of Israel, and his conduct was dictated by an overarching sense of responsibility toward both.

SPEAKING OF GOD

Ironically, as we will discuss later in this study guide, the God of Israel is not mentioned even once in the book of Esther. Yet He is mentioned twenty-two times in Ruth—seventeen times as *Yahweh* ("Lord"), three times as *Elohim* ("God"), and twice as *Sadday* ("Almighty"). In addition, the author of Ruth speaks of God's sovereign grace on two separate occasions, and eight different times various characters in the book mention the actions of God.

THE ULTIMATE MESSAGE

It's difficult to reduce the book of Ruth to one message, except for what we mentioned earlier. Beyond providing a marvelous call to all Christians, in all times and places, to trust God and act responsibly, the book of Ruth affirms the right of King David to the throne of Israel. In so doing it also establishes a clear line of succession, beginning with Abraham and extending to David, then on to Jesus Christ Himself through a total of forty-two separate generations (Matt. 1:1–17).

Ruth was redeemed by the grace of Boaz, and we in turn are redeemed by the grace of Jesus Christ. What a legacy for someone "grafted in" to the nation of Israel!

1

TO A NEW HOME

RUTH 1:1–22

Before We Begin . . .

What comes to mind when you think of the book of Ruth? What do you think it's really all about? Why do you think God wanted it in the Bible?

If you had to select a hero and a heroine from the book of Ruth, before working through this study, who would they be? Why?

ESTHER 1

The book of Ruth begins with an important bit of history, although it's very compressed. Let's see if we can sort it out by answering the following questions, all taken from the first five verses of chapter 1.

Where was Elimelech from? Based on that, what was his nationality—and that of his family?

What was his wife's name? What were the names of their two sons?

Where did Elimelech emigrate with his family—and why (v. 2)?

For extra credit: If the members of Elimelech's family were Ephrathites, what son of Jacob gave their tribe its name?

What were the names of the two Moabite women who married the sons of Elimelech and Naomi?

NAOMI RETURNS WITH RUTH

The first five verses of chapter 1 tell us that Naomi's husband, Elimelech, and their two sons died in Moab. But then things changed back in the land that the family of Elimelech came from in the first place.

What happened, according to verse 6? How did that development affect Naomi? (Hint: What does the text mean by "giving them bread"?)

Naomi was obviously from the tribe of Judah. By what name have all the people of the twelve tribes of Israel (i.e., the sons of Jacob) been known, down through the centuries, based on the name Judah?

WHAT DO WE KNOW ABOUT MOAB?

The nation of Moab, once located on the east side of the Dead Sea between Edom and Ammon, went out of existence centuries ago. The land it once occupied is now part of the country of Jordan.

Moab originated via the incestuous relationship between Lot and his oldest daughter, who "went in and lay with" her wine-drunk father (Gen. 19:30–38) to conceive a son, whom she named Moab. Moab is the same nation that refused to allow Moses and the children of Israel to pass through their portion of the land of Canaan on their roads. Ironically, Moses was buried in the land of Moab when he died, but that did very little to bring a lasting peace between the two nations. For a long time the Moabites and Israelites had an on-again, off-again kind of relationship—mostly off-again. Saul and David both fought the Moabites, and they were eventually conquered, if only temporarily, by Ehud.

During the time of Ruth, the Moabites and the Israelites were enjoying a period of relative tranquility. But a few centuries later, Moab plundered the land of the Israelites after they were defeated by Babylon. Moab later became part of the Babylon and Persian empires, at which time it disappeared as a separate entity.

The people of Moab were condemned by several biblical prophets for scoffing and boasting against Israel. They also were condemned for their pride, arrogance, and worship of idols.

Before her journey was fully under way, what did Naomi suggest to her two daughters-in-law? More importantly, why would she give them that particular word of advice?

What was their response (v. 10)?

WHY WERE HUSBANDS SO IMPORTANT?

To use a modern expression, in the ancient Hebrew culture, women were not completely disenfranchised. They had rights too. Indeed, one famous case involved a woman who divorced her camel-driver husband because he was gone so much he was physically unable to provide for her marriage rights.

Nevertheless, the man of the family was extremely important. Even though his wife probably contributed just as much physical labor as he did (and sometimes more!), it was the husband's sacred duty to protect and care for her, just as it then became his son's duty to care for his mother if the husband died first. The laws of inheritance reflected this emphasis. Though Moses made some obvious exceptions (most notably for the daughters of Zelophehad, who died with no male heirs; see Numbers 17:1–11) at God's leading, in most cases property was passed down through the generations through the male heirs.

This was especially true of land, the ancient Hebrew's primary source of wealth. Job was a rich man because he had a lot of land and many sons to work it—for land means food, and food supports animals and enterprises of all kinds. The same was true of Abraham and his nephew, Lot, and eventually of the children of Israel to whom God literally gave the land of Canaan.

We see the same emphasis repeated many generations later, in the book of Jeremiah, when the prophet admonished the captive Israelites in Babylon:

Build houses and dwell in them; plant gardens and eat their fruit. Take wives and beget sons and daughters; and take wives for your sons and give your daughters to husbands, so that they may bear sons and daughters—that you may be increased there, and not diminished. (Jer. 29:5–6 NKJV)

We also see the same dynamic working in God's choice of Jacob over Esau, for Jacob was willing to be a farmer, while Esau preferred hunting wild game—but that's another story! Our point here is that God established His people as a farming culture, destined to live peacefully off the produce of their land and the animals it supported.

But there was no way for a widow to live off her dead husband's property if she had no sons to inherit it, work it, and provide her a home. This conundrum was one of the major reasons for the kinsman redeemer laws talked about elsewhere in this study guide. And this is also what brought Ruth and Boaz together in such a noble, loving union, thus forming a major link in the ancestral chain leading to Christ Himself.

As you undoubtedly know (see the sidebar "Why Were Husbands So Important?" on page 9), Naomi was simply trying to make sure that her two daughters-in-law would be well established in their community through remarriage among their own people.

What was the likelihood that they'd be able to remarry if they returned to the land of Judah with Naomi?

Fill in the blanks in the following passage to understand Naomi's state of mind:

> But Naomi said, "Turn back, my _____; why will you go with me? Are there still sons in my womb, that they may be your _____? Turn back, my daughters, go—for I am too old to have a husband. If I should say I have hope, if I should have a husband tonight and should also bear _____, would you wait for them till they were grown? Would you _____ yourselves from having _____? No, my daughters; for it _____ me very much for your sakes that the hand of the Lord has gone out against me!" (Ruth 1:11–13 NKJV)

What was the difference between Ruth's behavior and Orpah's behavior (v. 14)?

Verses 16–17 contain what are undoubtedly the most famous words in the entire book of Ruth—and for some people might be the best-known words in the Bible. They have been used many times, in both exact repetitions and paraphrases, over the centuries. Indeed, they are almost part of our "common history," even though many people who use them, in one form or other, might not know where they came from—or to whom they were spoken.

Here they are:

> But Ruth said:
>
> "Entreat me not to leave you,
>
> Or to turn back from following after you;
>
> For wherever you go, I will go;
>
> And wherever you lodge, I will lodge;
>
> Your people shall be my people,
>
> And your God, my God.
>
> Where you die, I will die,
>
> And there will I be buried.
>
> The Lord do so to me, and more also,
>
> If anything but death parts you and me."
>
> (Ruth 1:16–17 NKJV)

What was Naomi's response (v. 18)?

To what city did the two women then travel? And what was the response of the people of that city when they arrived? In particular, what did the women say to Naomi?

Fill in the blanks in the following passage to see how Naomi responded:

> But she said to them, "Do not call me Naomi; call me _____, for the Almighty has dealt very _____ with me. I went out full, and the Lord has brought me _____ again empty. Why do you call me Naomi, since the Lord has _____ against me, and the Almighty has _____ me?" (Ruth 1:20–21 NKJV)

What important agricultural event in the lives of the people of Bethlehem was about to happen?

PULLING IT ALL TOGETHER . . .

• A severe famine in Judah motivated Elimelech to move from Bethlehem to the land of Moab. He went with his wife, Naomi, and their two sons, Mahlon and Chilion.

• Elimelech died in Moab. Meanwhile, his two sons grew up and married Moabite women, Ruth and Orpah.

• After about ten years, the two sons died as well, leaving Naomi and her two daughters-in-law alone, with no one to provide a living for them.

• Naomi then decided to return to the land of her birth, knowing that her chances of survival, as she aged, would be much better among her own people.

• At first, both of her daughters-in-law tried to go with her, but she was able to convince Orpah to stay in her own country. Ruth, however, would not let Naomi go alone, in her well-known "Entreat me not to leave you" speech.

• Thus Naomi and Ruth returned to Bethlehem at the beginning of the barley harvest.

WHY WERE NAMES SO IMPORTANT?

The ancient Hebrew aleph-bet (named for its first two letters, *aleph* and *bet*) was both pictographic and phonic. It was considered pictographic because each letter had its own built-in meanings—for example, the letter *gimel* meant "camel," and the letter *dalet* meant "door."

At the same time, Hebrew was also a phonetic language, meaning that it could be read by repeating the initial sounds of each letter, in right-to-left succession. Thus *gimel* would sound like an English *g*, and *dalet* would sound like a *d*. Taken together, these two characteristics made ancient Hebrew an incredibly rich language, capable of packing a whole universe of meanings into one short sentence—or even one word.

Names of people were prime examples. In a very real sense, a person "was" his or her name. And many times people even changed their names as their personalities changed during the course of their lifetimes. Or the change was made for them. Thus God Himself changed Abram's name to Abraham, Sarai's name to Sarah, and Jacob's name to Israel, each of which He changed for a specific reason. And thus Moses' father-in-law changed his own name from Reuel to Jethro ("Abundance") after Moses married his daughter—perhaps because he felt elevated (and potentially enriched) by his daughter's marriage to a man who'd grown up in the Egyptian pharaoh's court.

In the book of Ruth, these names had the following meanings. How well does each one reflect the character of its owner?

Ruth (Friend)
Naomi (Pleasant One)
Boaz (In Him is Strength)
Elimelech (God is My King)
Mahlon (Sick)
Chilion (Pining)
Bethlehem (House of Bread)

2

GOD PROVIDES

RUTH 2:1–23

Before We Begin . . .

What was the meaning of the word "glean" in biblical times? What was the established custom among the ancient Hebrews, and who established it?

Have you ever seen anything similar in modern times in the farmlands of America? In industry? In public service professions?

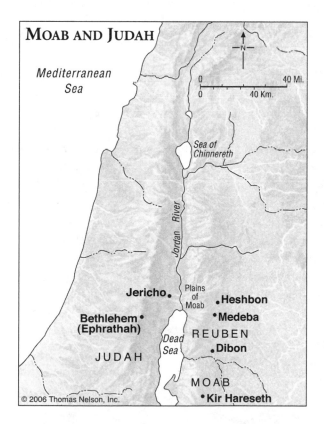

What Was a Kinsman Redeemer?

The word for "kinsman redeemer" in Hebrew is *goel*—meaning "to redeem," "to receive," or "to buy back." As with several other concepts (most notably the various covenants) that were familiar to the children of Israel since before the days of Abraham, the details are not all given in one place in the Bible. And some are not given at all and have to be extracted from other contemporary sources.

In this case, the general concept of a kinsman redeemer is first introduced in the book of Leviticus:

> *"After he is sold he may be redeemed again. One of his brothers may redeem him; or his uncle or his uncle's son may redeem him; or anyone who is near of kin to him in his family may redeem him." (Lev. 25:48–49 NKJV)*

In this particular instance, the text refers to God's provision for a poor person who had been forced to sell something he owned—or even himself into slavery. Always, his nearest of kin (i.e., his kinsman redeemer) had the right to step forward and buy back what his relative had been forced to sell.

In effect, a kinsman redeemer was a related-by-blood benefactor capable of freeing the debtor by paying the ransom price.

> *"If one of your brethren becomes poor, and has sold some of his possession, and if his redeeming relative comes to redeem it, then he may redeem what his brother sold." (Lev. 25:25 NKJV)*

This concept is further elaborated in the book of Ruth itself, via the words of Boaz when he spoke to the relative who was more closely related to Ruth than he himself:

> *"And I thought to inform you, saying, 'Buy it [Naomi's land] back in the presence of the inhabitants and the elders of my people. If you will redeem it, redeem it; but if you will not redeem it, then tell me, that I may know; for there is no one but you to redeem it, and I am next after you.'" (Ruth 4:4 NKJV)*

The kinsman redeemer could function in any of the following ways:

- If a family member died without an heir, the kinsman redeemer could perpetuate that person's name by marrying the widow and rearing a son to pass down the family name (Gen. 38:8; Deut. 25:5; Ruth 3–4). This is exactly what Boaz did for Ruth.

- When death came at the hands of another man, the kinsman redeemer could act as the "avenger of blood" and pursue the killer (Num. 35:12–34; Deut. 19:1–3).
- The kinsman redeemer concept is used in reference to things consecrated to God (Lev. 27:13–31), to God as the Redeemer of His people (Exod. 6:6; Isa. 43:1; 44:22; 48:20; 49:7), and to those redeemed by God (Isa. 35:9; 51:10; Job 19:25).
- The right of redemption (and thus the "office" of kinsman redeemer) belonged to the nearest kinsman, but could then be passed down the line (Lev. 25:25), as it was in the book of Ruth, between Boaz and the unnamed closer relative who declined the honor.

A true kinsman redeemer had to satisfy three basic requirements:

1. He must be *near of kin* (Lev. 25:48; 25:25; Ruth 3:12–13).
2. He must be *able* to redeem (Ruth 4:4–6).
3. He must be *willing* to redeem (Ruth 4:6ff.).

Redemption was only complete when the price was completely paid. This concept, along with all those we've introduced above, is further expanded upon throughout the book of Ruth. In fact, many scholars look at Ruth in its entirety and see the following biblical "types":

- Naomi left the land and went out to exile, thus picturing Israel's departure from God.
- Ruth is a picture of the Gentile bride of Christ.
- Boaz is a picture of Christ, the ultimate Kinsman Redeemer.
- The relative of Boaz who declined to redeem Ruth is a picture of the law, which cannot redeem anyone by itself.

In contrast, Job (whose troubles are detailed in his own book) complained that no one came to redeem him when his difficulties began. Even so, he demonstrated his faith by proclaiming that Yahweh would provide His kinsman redeemer: "For I know that my Redeemer lives, and He shall stand at last on the earth" (Job 19:25 NKJV).

God, of course, is the ultimate Kinsman Redeemer of His people. When they lost their liberty in Egypt, He rescued them from bondage. "I am the Lord . . . I will redeem you with an outstretched arm and with great judgments" (Exod. 6:6 NKJV). And, of course, Christ Himself will redeem all of His own at the end of this age. (For more on this subject, see "Kinsman Redeemer Revisited" in chapter 4 of this study guide.)

RUTH 2

Almost everything that happened in the rest of the book of Ruth, beginning with the events detailed in 2:2, has to be understood within the context of the "kinsman redeemer" custom of biblical times. If you are not fully familiar with this tradition, please read the sidebar "What Was a Kinsman Redeemer?" in this chapter to gain a fuller understanding before you read further in the book of Ruth.

RUTH MEETS BOAZ

Ruth's comments in verse 1 tell us that she is already thinking of the best way to secure her future, according to ancient Israelite custom.

What did she say that indicated what was on her mind (v. 2)?

What does Boaz's greeting to his reapers suggest to us about his character and his relationship—good or bad—with the God of Israel? Based on what you know of Ruth's and Naomi's intentions, does this imply good or bad for them?

What was the general attitude of Boaz's workers toward Ruth? Were they protective and respectful, or were they disdainful?

What is the essence of what Boaz tells Ruth in verses 8–9?

What was Ruth's reaction?

Boaz's response in 2:11 reemphasizes something very important about Ruth, which was first made clear in her well-known
speech to Naomi ("Your people shall be my people, and your
God, my God" [Ruth 1:16 NKJV]). The same important truth
might also be inferred from her actions. But beyond all that,
Boaz told her, "The Lord repay your work, and a full reward
be given you by the Lord God of Israel, under whose wings
you have come for refuge" (2:12 NKJV).

In other words, Boaz is fully aware that Ruth now worships
the God of Israel and has effectively been "grafted in" (in
modern terminology) to the children of Israel. In effect,
though she was once a Moabitess, she is now an Israelite.

*Nonetheless, what do you believe Ruth meant when she said, "I
am not like one of your maidservants" (v. 13 NKJV)? In what
way might Ruth have been different from Boaz's other maidservants?*

Fill in the blanks in the passage below to see how Boaz further
responds to Ruth:

> *Now Boaz said to her at _____, "Come here, and
> eat of the _____, and dip your piece of bread in
> the _____." So she sat beside the reapers, and he
> passed parched grain to her; and she ate and was satis-
> fied, and kept some back. And when she rose up to
> _____, Boaz commanded his young men, saying,
> "Let her glean even among the sheaves, and do not
> _____ her. Also let grain from the bundles fall*

_____ *for her; leave it that she may glean, and do not rebuke her." (Ruth 2:14–16 NKJV)*

What modern "dipping" custom—especially prevalent in Italian restaurants!—do we observe today that is identical to what Boaz told Ruth to do?

How much barley did Ruth glean after she'd beaten the grains from the stalks (v. 17)?

An ephah of barley was about half a bushel and weighed about thirty pounds. This much grain was actually quite a bit for one gleaner to gather in one day and would be enough food for one person for several days.

WHAT IS "PARCHED GRAIN"?

When Boaz invited Ruth to eat with him, part of the meal included roasted or "parched" barley. The ancient Israelites parched kernels of barley by heating them on an iron plate over an open fire. The kernels then developed a toasty taste and texture, and could be eaten "out of hand" somewhat like popcorn, although they did not "pop" and expand in the same way.

Also, Boaz invited Ruth to dip her bread in vinegar, another ancient mealtime custom that has seen a recent renaissance. This is especially true in Italian restaurants that invite patrons to dip hot bread into small platters of olive oil mixed with exotic vinegars.

What did Ruth then do with what she'd collected?

Verses 19–23 provide additional details that help us understand what was happening. Boaz certainly had a favorable reaction to Ruth! He not only invited her to eat with him, but he also gave her explicit permission to glean "even among the sheaves." This meant she did not need to wait until his own workers had finished in a given field; neither did she need to stay near the outer edges. She was welcome to pick up fallen grain among Boaz's main portion of the harvest even as his workers were gathering it in.

Also, Boaz told her not to worry about drawing her own water if she became thirsty; he gave her explicit permission to drink from the water already drawn for his workers and to be very much at home among his own servant girls. We know that Boaz was about Naomi's age, and thus Ruth was undoubtedly much younger. But she was obviously an attractive woman, and Boaz knew she would be safer if she were nearer the center of action, among his own workers, not on the outskirts where others might take unfair advantage of her.

What did Naomi tell Ruth about Boaz (v. 20)? Was this new information, or was Naomi simply repeating what Ruth already knew?

Fill in the blanks in these verses to learn more about how things went with Ruth over the next several months, during the barley harvest (March–April) and then the wheat harvest (June–July):

And Naomi said to Ruth her daughter-in-law, "It is
_____*, my daughter, that you go out with his*
young _____*, and that people do not* _____
you in any other field." So she stayed close by the young
_____ *of Boaz, to glean until the end of*
_____ *harvest and* _____ *harvest; and she*
dwelt with her _____*. (Ruth 2:22–23 NKJV)*

PULLING IT ALL TOGETHER . . .

• Naomi's dead husband had a rich relative named Boaz. When Ruth asked Naomi for permission to glean in Boaz's fields, Naomi was only too happy to give her permission.

• As soon as Boaz saw Ruth and realized who she was, he treated her with extreme care and concern. He told her to stay close to his own servants and to drink from the water drawn for his own workers. He also told the young men in the fields not to touch her, and then he invited her to lunch.

• When Ruth asked Boaz why he was being so kind to her, he explained that he'd heard of how she'd left her own country to come to Israel with Naomi and care for her.

• Ruth gleaned quite a bit of grain on that first day. That night, once she'd told Naomi her story, Naomi realized that a good thing was happening!

3

LOVE REDEEMS

RUTH 3:1–18

Before We Begin . . .

If you have read the book of Ruth before, what did you think Ruth meant by uncovering Boaz's feet while he slept?

Can you think of anything in our modern culture that might have derived from this ancient understanding?

RUTH 3

This chapter begins with a clear directive from Naomi to Ruth, telling her exactly what to do, in accord with Jewish tradition, to avail herself of the kinsman redeemer law.

What did Naomi tell Ruth she sought for her (v. 1)?

What did Naomi say that Boaz would be doing that very night (v. 2)?

Under the Wings of Your Garment

Ruth 2:12 reads, "The Lord repay your work, and a full reward be given you by the Lord God of Israel, under whose wings you have come for refuge" (NKJV).

In this passage, the word "wings" comes from the Hebrew word *kanaf*, which can also be translated "corners," as of a garment. By itself this word might not seem to have any deeper meaning, but the image it brings forth actually has profound implications that stretch all the way from the beginning of the Old Testament through the New Testament and beyond.

When an ancient Hebrew man married his wife, at the end of the wedding ceremony he would draw the corners of his outer garment over her head, symbolically covering her with his protection. But the corners of that garment, called a *talit* (also spelled *tallit* and sometimes *tallis*, and generally translated in modern English as "prayer shawl"), had additional symbolic meaning beyond their function as a covering.

The four corners of an ancient Hebrew man's outer garment also contained what modern translations often call a "fringe." But this so-called fringe was not like a modern fringe that we might see on the edge of an Oriental rug or on the sleeves of a biker jacket. On the contrary, the ancient Hebrews were commanded by God to wear what the New King James Version calls "tassels" on the corners of their garments to remind them constantly of Him:

> Again the Lord spoke to Moses, saying, "Speak to the children of Israel: Tell them to make tassels on the corners of their garments throughout their generations, and to put a blue thread in the tassels of the corners. And you shall have the tassel, that you may look upon it and remember all the commandments of the Lord and do them, and that you may not follow the harlotry to which your own heart and your own eyes are inclined, and that you may remember and do all My commandments, and be holy for your God. I am the Lord your God, who brought you out of the land of Egypt, to be your God: I am the Lord your God." (Num. 15:37–41 NKJV)

The "tassels" in the above translation were known to the ancient Hebrews as *tzit-tzit*. Each one was made of four long threads, one of which was dyed blue to represent God. All four were looped through a hole in the corner of the garment and "doubled down," thus providing eight separate threads. Four of these were then wrapped around the other four in a numerical pattern and set permanently in place by knots, with the numbers of each group of wrappings corresponding to the numbers/letters of the aleph-bet that spelled *YHWH*, the name of God (which we often translate "Jehovah" even though ancient Hebrew had no *j* sound).

Thus when a Hebrew man prayed, he would wrap the tzit-tzit around his fingers to have the name of God "in his hand." And when he covered his bride with his "wings," he was simultaneously covering her with the name of God.

Do you understand now the multilayered symbolism of what Ruth did when she went to Boaz and literally put herself under the wings of his (and God's) protection?

What do you think it means to "winnow barley"? Why would that even be necessary?

What was Naomi's advice to Ruth?

What was the last thing Naomi told Ruth to do? Based on the material in the sidebar "Under the Wings of Your Garment," why did Naomi give Ruth this advice?

What was Ruth's response (v. 5)?

Fill in the blanks below to get all the details:

So she went down to the _____ floor and did according to all that her mother-in-law instructed her. And after Boaz had eaten and drunk, and his heart was _____, he went to _____ down at the end of the heap of grain; and she came softly, uncovered his feet, and lay down. (Ruth 3:6–7 NKJV)

What happened to Boaz at midnight (v. 8)?

Pay special attention to what Ruth said in response to Boaz's question (v. 9). To take someone "under your wing" is now a common expression, meaning to care for that person. However, based on what you learned from the sidebar "Under the Wings of Your Garment," what was the deeper meaning in Ruth's gesture?

Fill in the blanks in the following passage to see how Boaz responded:

Then he said, "Blessed are you of the Lord, my _____! For you have shown more _____ at the end than at the _____, in that you did not go after _____ men, whether poor or rich. And now, my daughter, do not fear. I will do for you all that you request, for all the people of my town know that you are a virtuous woman." (Ruth 3:10–11 NKJV)

How would you characterize Boaz's response in the above passage? What three things (at the very minimum) can you discern about him from what he said?

What did Boaz mean by "perform the duty" (v. 13)? Again—based on your understanding of what you have already read—to what ancient custom was Boaz referring?

Ruth now went back to sleep, only to rise early in the morning while it was still too dark for anyone to realize that she'd even been there. But did she awaken entirely by herself?

What did Boaz then ask her to do? In a somewhat indirect way, how does his expression "the shawl that is on you" reinforce what we already know about his and Ruth's sense of honor toward each other?

WINGS OF ANOTHER DIMENSION . . .

Carefully read all we have said about tzit-tzit and "wings" as background, and then fast-forward to what Christ Himself said when He entered Jerusalem just before His Crucifixion:

> *"O Jerusalem, Jerusalem, the one who kills the prophets and stones those who are sent to her! How often I wanted to gather your children together, as a hen gathers her chicks under her wings, but you were not willing!" (Matt. 23:37 NKJV)*

Though the literal image of a hen covering her chicks is certainly valid, at a deeper level Christ was speaking very clearly—to the ancient Hebrews who understood the symbolism—of His heartfelt desire to gather and protect His people as a groom protects his bride.

Other "winged references" to the same concept appear in Psalms 17:8; 36:7; 61:4; 63:7; and 91:4.

And yes, the "fringe" touched by the woman with an issue of blood (Matt. 9:20) was undoubtedly the tzit-tzit on Christ's outer garment, just as those same tzit-tzit were almost assuredly the "hem of his garment" mentioned in other places in English translations of the Bible. Also, when Christ resurrected the little girl (daughter of Jairus) from death, He spoke what most English translations render as . . . Well, here's the verse:

> *Then He took the child by the hand, and said to her, "Talitha, cumi," which is translated, "Little girl, I say to you, arise." (Mark 5:41 NKJV)*

A better translation of "Talitha, cumi" (a Hebrew expression, incidentally, that calls into question the common assumption that Christ spoke Aramaic instead of biblical Hebrew) might be, "Little girl in the talit, arise!" Most likely, since only Hebrew men were buried in their talits, Christ wrapped the girl in His own prayer shawl before He brought her back to life.

This is not to suggest, of course, that ancient prayer shawls and fringes by themselves—even those worn by Christ—had any redemptive or healing power of their own. Yet it is very likely that they were used by Him to facilitate His purposes on more than one occasion.

What did Boaz give Ruth to take home to Naomi?

After Naomi heard Ruth's account of what had happened so far, was her reaction positive or negative?

How do you think she could be so sure that Boaz would not rest until he had "concluded the matter this day" (v. 18)?

PULLING IT ALL TOGETHER . . .

• Naomi gave Ruth specific instructions about what to do on the night when Boaz was winnowing barley. Basically, she told Ruth to let Boaz know by her actions that she desired him to be her kinsman redeemer.

• After Boaz had lain down to sleep on the threshing floor (to protect his grain while it was still out in the open), Ruth uncovered his feet and lay down herself, symbolically inviting him to redeem her by marrying her and giving her legitimate children to carry on the family name.

• Boaz was mightily impressed and blessed Ruth for her integrity—for not going after younger men but instead honoring the long-established customs of his people.

• Boaz then promised to marry Ruth if the one man who had legal precedence over him refused the honor.

Reward and Conclusion

4

Ruth 4:1–21

Before We Begin ...

How does the concept of marrying someone only to produce a male heir strike you? Is there anything comparable in our society today? What about countries that still retain monarchies, such as England or Sweden?

If you had to give a prize to the one person most responsible for the marriage of Ruth and Boaz, to whom would you give it?

Ruth 4

We now see a graphic demonstration of the kinsman redeemer law in action.

Read through the opening verses of Ruth 4, included below, then answer the questions that follow:

> *Now Boaz went up to the gate and sat down there; and behold, the close relative of whom Boaz had spoken came by. So Boaz said, "Come aside, friend, sit down here." So he came aside and sat down. And he took ten men of the elders of the city, and said, "Sit down here." So they sat down. Then he said to the close relative, "Naomi, who has come back from the country of Moab, sold the piece of land which belonged to our brother Elimelech. And I thought to inform you, saying, 'Buy it back in the presence of the inhabitants and the elders of my people. If you will redeem it, redeem it; but if you will not redeem it, then tell me, that I may know; for there is no one but you to redeem it, and I am next after you.'"*

And he said, "I will redeem it."

Then Boaz said, "On the day you buy the field from the hand of Naomi, you must also buy it from Ruth the Moabitess, the wife of the dead, to perpetuate the name of the dead through his inheritance."

And the close relative said, "I cannot redeem it for myself, lest I ruin my own inheritance. You redeem my right of redemption for yourself, for I cannot redeem it." (Ruth 4:1–6 NKJV)

WHY THE SANDAL EXCHANGE?

Ruth 4:7 says, "Now this was the custom in former times in Israel concerning redeeming and exchanging, to confirm anything: one man took off his sandal and gave it to the other, and this was a confirmation in Israel" (NKJV).

What this verse does not give us is the derivation of this custom. It dates back to the days of Abraham and beyond, and it refers to the third of the four established covenants that the ancient Hebrews could enter into with each other. Known as inheritance (or "sandal") covenant—and pretty much a given between father and son once the father's blessing had been bestowed—it was symbolized by the positioning of used sandals, held down by rocks, at the four corners of a person's land. These were sacred boundary markers that could not be moved by anyone, for they marked the corners of the next generation's inheritance. Here is what God had to say about them:

"You shall not remove your neighbor's landmark, which the men of old have set, in your inheritance which you will inherit in the land the Lord your God is giving you to possess." (Deut. 19:14 NKJV)

Incidentally, Christ was referring both to sandal covenant and to marriage covenant (the highest two) when he removed His disciples' sandals and washed their feet, in John 13:4–8, just as an ancient Hebrew groom did for his wife at their wedding.

Why did Boaz go to the gate of the city to conduct his business? What was so special about that particular place?

Once he'd made contact with the man he sought, why did Boaz then ask ten elders of the city to sit with them as well? What was their function in the upcoming scenario?

Boaz then indicated that Naomi needed to sell a piece of land that had once belonged to her husband, Elimelech. We are not told how she acquired it, and we can only presume that she was selling it because she had no other source of income. The relative Boaz was addressing had to be given an opportunity to exercise his right to buy the land and keep it in the family (i.e., his first right of refusal to "redeem" it, which was his because he was even closer by blood to Naomi than Boaz was).

But the situation wasn't quite that simple, for Boaz's mention of Ruth, whom the kinsman redeemer would be required to redeem by buying the land, suggests that the original piece of property had passed from Elimelech to Mahlon, Ruth's deceased husband, before Mahlon died. Thus the kinsman redeemer, by buying the land and "redeeming" it from non-family ownership, would also acquire the responsibility to marry Ruth and give her a male descendant, who would then carry on the Elimelech/Mahlon name as the eventual property owner.

LEVIRATE MARRIAGE AND KINSMAN REDEMPTION—WHICH IS WHICH?

It is sometimes difficult for modern readers to fully understand all the dynamics of the Boaz-Ruth-Naomi relationship as it developed through the book of Ruth. This is true for two reasons:

1. First, as we have mentioned elsewhere in this study guide, modern students of the Bible, without a certain amount of independent study, are simply not familiar with many of the cultural concepts that held the ancient Hebrew society together—in some cases in a very *literal* sense.

2. Second, in the interactions between Ruth, Boaz, Naomi, and the unnamed kinsman who declined his right of kinsman redemption, we are actually dealing with two interrelated yet different concepts: kinsman redemption and levirate marriage (also sometimes spelled *levirite*).

Strictly speaking, the marriage between Ruth and Boaz was not an example of a levirate marriage. Rather, as most commentators correctly assert, when Ruth let Boaz know (by uncovering his feet—see "Under the Wings of Your Garment" in chapter 3 of this study guide) that she would prefer marrying him to pursuing a younger man, she was inviting him to marry her as her kinsman redeemer. Boaz understood this instantly and responded as follows:

> Then he said, "Blessed are you of the Lord, my daughter! For you have shown more kindness at the end than at the beginning, in that you did not go after young men, whether poor or rich. And now, my daughter, do not fear. I will do for you all that you request, for all the people of my town know that you are a virtuous woman. Now it is true that I am a close relative; however, there is a relative closer than I. Stay this night, and in the morning it shall be that if he will perform the duty of a close relative for you—good; let him do it. But if he does not want to perform the duty for you, then I will perform the duty for you, as the Lord lives! Lie down until morning." (Ruth 3:10–13 NKJV)

In the next chapter of Ruth, when Boaz spoke to the unnamed relative, we quickly see that he knew a good deal more about the situation than we, the readers, have been told up to that point. Boaz explained the following facts to the relative:

1. Naomi has a piece of property she wants to sell.

2. Ruth also has ownership in the same property. However, on this point the details are not 100 percent clear. Some commentators suggest that perhaps the land originally belonged to Elimelech, Naomi's husband, then passed down to Ruth's husband at Elimelech's death, then back to Naomi-Ruth at the death of the son.

Regardless of the details, at least one thing is certain. When Boaz spoke of "duty" in the above passage, he was speaking of his right (which he considered a duty) as a kinsman redeemer to buy the land, marry Ruth, give her a male heir (if possible), and also be responsible for the welfare of Naomi if the funds from the sale of the land ever failed to be sufficient.

In contrast, here is the biblical passage that best defines the ancient institution of levirate marriage, which is the other somewhat similar cultural institution with which kinsman redemption sometimes gets confused:

"If brothers dwell together, and one of them dies and has no son, the widow of the dead man shall not be married to a stranger outside the family; her husband's brother shall go in to her, take her as his wife, and perform the duty of a husband's brother to her. And it shall be that the firstborn son which she bears will succeed to the name of his dead brother, that his name may not be blotted out of Israel. But if the man does not want to take his brother's wife, then let his brother's wife go up to the gate to the elders, and say, 'My husband's brother refuses to raise up a name to his brother in Israel; he will not perform the duty of my husband's brother.' Then the elders of his city shall call him and speak to him. But if he stands firm and says, 'I do not want to take her,' then his brother's wife shall come to him in the presence of the elders, remove his sandal from his foot, spit in his face, and answer and say, 'So shall it be done to the man who will not build up his brother's house.' And his name shall be called in Israel, 'The house of him who had his sandal removed.' "
(Deut. 25:5–10 NKJV)

Finally, one additional comment on this subject. This business of removing the sandal from the foot of a man who refused to marry his brother's wife is also related to the concept of sandal (inheritance) covenant. As we have mentioned elsewhere, sandals were used to mark the property boundaries of ancient Hebrew land parcels. Thus the heirs would inherit what was "between the sandals." Likewise, sandals were used in the marriage ceremony, during which the bridegroom washed his new wife's feet and put new sandals on them, signifying her "ownership" of all that was his.

However, this custom was symbolic, for in a legal sense they were married even before the ceremony. Thus even if the bridegroom died prior to the marriage ceremony, as long as they'd signed a marriage contract, they were legally married. In effect, the contract brought them together *legally,* while the ceremony completed the union by bringing them together *physically, emotionally,* and *spiritually.*

Perhaps most fascinating of all to modern Christians (and further proof that the Bible is one unified book from cover to cover, written by only one God), as also mentioned elsewhere, we see Christ doing the same thing for His disciples at the Last Supper. He even told Peter that he could not inherit the kingdom of God unless he allowed Christ to perform this symbolic act, which connected so directly to both the ancient inheritance covenant and to marriage itself.

In any case, given all the above, it should be very clear that a woman who took off her sandal and spit in her husband's brother's face was giving him the ultimate public reproach!

Unfortunately for the first-option kinsman, however, because he already had property and probably a son (or sons) of his own, he realized instantly that marrying Ruth and giving her male children could complicate his own estate. Indeed, it could even result in some of his current property passing on to Ruth's offspring someday, thus diminishing the estate that his own existing son(s) would inherit.

So he had second thoughts, changed his mind, and thus passed on the right of redemption to Boaz.

As we have further explained in the sidebar "Why the Sandal Exchange?" what did the unnamed relative then do (vv. 7–8)?

At that point, Boaz and the elders of the people who were assembled with him at the city gate had the following exchange:

And Boaz said to the elders and all the people, "You are witnesses this day that I have bought all that was Elimelech's, and all that was Chilion's and Mahlon's, from the hand of Naomi. Moreover, Ruth the Moabitess, the widow of Mahlon, I have acquired as my wife, to perpetuate the name of the dead through his inheritance, that the name of the dead may not be cut off from among his brethren and from his position at the gate. You are witnesses this day."

And all the people who were at the gate, and the elders, said, "We are witnesses. The Lord make the woman who is coming to your house like Rachel and Leah, the two who built the house of Israel; and may you prosper in Ephrathah and be famous in Bethlehem. May your house be like the house of Perez, whom Tamar bore to Judah, because of the offspring which the Lord will give you from this young woman." (Ruth 4:9–12 NKJV)

And so the story of Ruth and Boaz draws to a close, with just a few more questions about what happened after they were married.

What was the reaction of the women of Bethlehem toward Naomi when Ruth bore the son of Boaz (vv. 13–14)?

What was that son's name? Who was his son? And who eventually became his grandson?

Thus the direct line from Abraham, Isaac, and Jacob was established through Ruth to David and thence to Christ Himself.

KINSMAN REDEEMER REVISITED

Many commentators see the book of Ruth in highly symbolic terms. For example, some think of Naomi as a picture of Israel—one who, like the ancient Israelites, wandered away from Bethlehem (i.e., Israel, the land of her spiritual ancestry) but eventually returned.

Ruth, of course, is a picture of the nation of Israel as she should have been down through the centuries—honest, sincere, filled with integrity, and eager to worship God without reservation. But most of all, she was also willing to *trust* Him and His ability to provide by doing exactly what He had long since established by law as the honorable, proper conduct for a young widow.

And Boaz, of course, most closely resembles Christ Himself, the honorable Kinsman Redeemer, ready and willing to redeem Ruth (us) at a moment's notice, based on even the subtlest signs that we truly desire a redemptive relationship with Him.

PULLING IT ALL TOGETHER . . .

• Boaz went to the city gates, where he knew he would find the elders of the city and a willing audience, so that he could conduct his business with the close relative who had what we might call "first right of refusal" to redeem Naomi's property and marry Ruth.

• This relative at first agreed to buy the property. But as soon as he realized that he would also be obligated to marry Ruth and give her a son, whose eventual inheritance might include some of his own previously held property, the close relative bowed out.

• He took off his sandal and gave it to Boaz, symbolically passing the redemption right to Boaz. And because all the elders saw and heard what had happened, it was entirely legal.

• Boaz then bought the property, married Ruth, and produced a son named Obed. Obed had a son named Jesse, and Jesse was David's father. Thus Ruth, a non-Jew from Moab, became the great-grandmother of David.

5

COMING TO A CLOSE

It is hard to overstate the importance of obedience to God's laws. Throughout the Bible we are given clear examples of what happens to those who obeyed God as closely as they were able and reaped benefits beyond measure as a result. Saul, David, and especially David's son, Solomon, are all brilliant examples. But so are Abraham, Deborah, Moses, Joshua, Gideon, Jephthah, Paul, Noah, eleven of the twelve disciples, and many others.

At the same time, it's possible to examine the lives of most of the above and see precisely what happened when they began to disobey. Solomon is one of the more obvious examples, a man to whom God gave untold wisdom and wealth until Solomon began to turn away from Him to worship the pagan idols of his wives and concubines. Likewise, Saul, Judas, and most of the others are not far behind. Even Moses, admittedly held to a higher standard than anyone else because of his high leadership position, lost the right to set foot in the Promised Land before he died because of a temper tantrum years earlier that God simply could not overlook.

And then we have Ruth and Boaz. Not all the characters in their story display the kind of willing obedience to God's code of conduct that each of these two demonstrated. But perhaps the irresponsibility of Elimelech—and the bitterness of Naomi, however fleeting—can serve to highlight the clarity of Ruth and Boaz's devotion to the God of Israel.

Each one did exactly the right thing at the right time. Each one also demonstrated a profound willingness to give up personal pleasures to help someone else. But most important, each one gave full credit to God for every blessing they received and every good thing they saw in the lives of others. Thus Boaz recognized the hand of God in Ruth's life long before he married her. And thus Ruth and Naomi both knew instinctively that Boaz was "the real thing" who worshiped the real God, and not a pious hypocrite.

Perhaps this is the ultimate lesson for all of us from the book of Ruth. There simply is no substitute for total devotion to God, infusing every aspect of our hearts and minds, in every moment of our daily lives.

And there simply is no substitute for what God can do for us if we give Him that kind of unreserved worship and love.

ESTHER

INTRODUCTION

To untold generations of Jewish people—religious or secular, orthodox or conservative, Israeli citizens or those dispersed in some other country—the book of Esther is among the most familiar and the most beloved in their entire Bible. Certainly it is not a book of doctrine; certainly it cannot be used to extrapolate even a single brand-new mitzvah (although it illustrates several that God had already established; see the sidebar "*Mitvah* or *Mitzvot?*"); and certainly the rumor you've probably heard is true.

It doesn't mention God *even once!*

Even so, the book of Esther is like the ultimate Jewish success story. It's one in which all the elements of all the classic tales of Jewish survival down through the centuries, from the Crusades of the Middle Ages to the twentieth-century atrocities of Hitler to the establishment of their own state, come together to say, once and for all, that no matter how hard you try, you simply cannot eradicate God's chosen people from the face of the earth!

It's also a relatively simple story—clear, cogent, straightforward, impossible to misinterpret. Bad guy tries to kill Jews. Jewish heroine steps up to the plate. Jewish grandmother (in this case, a male cousin!) offers encouragement and advice. Bad guy loses; suffers precisely the punishment he tried to bring about for the leader of the Jewish community, who simply wanted to get along.

Beyond all that, however, the book of Esther is also the ultimate success story for all of God's people. For this, of course, is the magnificent subtext that undergirds everything we read in the entire book. Whatever the reason, the writer of this book chose not to mention God; but both God's love and His ability to protect His chil-

MITZVAH OR MITZVOT?

In the first five books of the Bible God gave the Jews a total of 613 *mitzvot* (*mitzvah* in the singular form). These are often referred to separately as commandments and collectively as "the Law."

However, as we have detailed in other study guides within this series, the Ten Commandments were clearly commandments, but many of the remaining 603 mitzvot were more in the form of *guidelines for righteous living*. And of those 603, only about 180 are still applicable today, because the rest involved do's and don'ts relating to the sacrificial system, which was done away with by the Romans' destruction of the temple in AD 70.

With respect to the "keeping of the (remaining) mitzvot" among the Jews, they take a unique approach to that whole subject that helps explain why they have survived as a distinct people group for more than two thousand years of dispersion. Everyone acknowledges that no one can keep all the mitzvot by himself, for no one is perfect. But as a group, with one keeping two or three and someone else keeping another two or three, at any given moment it is at least possible for the Jewish people to be correctly observing all 603 (or, more correctly, in modern times all 180 or so) of the mitzvot—but only as a *group*.

What is impossible for one person by himself is quite possible for all the people together, and this point of view is one of those intangibles that has made the Jews who they are. Even today, if a Jew is questioned about why he or she is caring for a penniless widow by taking food packages to her or paying her heating bills, he will tell you, "It's a mitzvot!"

And for devout Jews (and some not-so-devout Jews as well!), that says it all. In their own words, with *Torah* used as an equivalent for *mitzvot*, the Jews have not retained their identity by keeping the Torah. On the contrary, the Torah has kept the Jews.

dren, no matter how dire the circumstances, shine through in every line. At the same time, at another level the book of Esther teaches us that God sometimes works in ways that are not so obvious. He can even work in ways that *seem* to be coincidence, chance, or plain old good luck.

But we know better, for these are not secular Jewish characters, acting out their life stories without the slightest consideration for what God would direct them to do. These are quintessential God-fearing, God-worshiping people acting exactly as we know He would have them act. They trust Him to bring about the right result *if they do the right thing.*

And that is why the book of Esther is for everyone—Jews and Gentiles of all races and in all times and places. But let us pause for a moment and put the book itself into historical perspective before we extract any more of its lessons.

HISTORICAL SETTING

The events in the book of Esther occurred over a ten-year period, beginning in 483 BC and extending to 473 BC. We know that King Ahasuerus (Xerxes) came to power in 485 BC, and held the reins until his assassination in 465 BC. Thus we get the first date from the following passage:

> *Now it came to pass in the days of Ahasuerus (this was the Ahasuerus who reigned over one hundred and twenty-seven provinces, from India to Ethiopia), in those days when King Ahasuerus sat on the throne of his kingdom, which was in Shushan the citadel, that in the third year of his reign he made a feast for all his officials and servants—the powers of Persia and Media, the nobles, and the princes of the provinces being before him. (Esther 1:1–3 NKJV)*

We get the second date from this passage:

> *In the first month, which is the month of Nisan, in the twelfth year of King Ahasuerus, they cast Pur (that is, the lot), before Haman to determine the day and the month, until it fell on the twelfth month, which is the month of Adar. (Esther 3:7 NKJV)*

The word "they" in the verse above refers to the servants of King Ahasuerus. Haman, of course, was the bad guy referenced earlier. Perhaps needless to say, once the lots had been cast (see the sidebar "Where Does the Word *Purim* Come From?" in chapter 9), the remaining events in the book of Esther took place very quickly, most likely within a matter of days.

The historical period in which all of this happened was what is sometimes called the "Persian Period," extending roughly from 539 BC to 331 BC. The Israelites had been freed from captivity in Babylon, and many had returned from exile to rebuild the temple and reestablish the sacrificial system, as told in the books of Ezra and Nehemiah.

However, many Jews had *not* left Babylon and its environs, including the group to which Esther and Mordecai belonged.

MAIN CHARACTERS AND SETTING

The man whom some biblical translations (including the New King James Version) call King Ahasuerus was better known in history as Xerxes, the Persian ruler who succeeded his father, Darius. Xerxes reigned in "Shushan the citadel" (Esther 1:3 NKJV), meaning the Persian palace in the city of Shushan, which was on the east side of the Tigris River and about 150 miles north of the Persian Gulf, in what is now southwestern Iran. (Note that people from Iran were known in the United States as "Persians" until the 1970s and '80s.)

Shushan, which seems to have been the setting for all the events in the book of Esther, is now the city of Shush. However, Xerxes also reigned from another palace in Persepolis during the summer—the Shushan citadel was his winter palace.

It's also worth noting that the Shushan citadel burned down sometime during the reign of Xerxes' son, Artaxerxes, who succeeded his father about eleven years after the final event in the book of Esther. Thus someone writing from a much later time might not have known about Shushan, which suggests that the writer probably lived during a time period fairly close to the events in question—and perhaps concurrently.

With reference to the woman we call Esther, most commentators agree that Hadassah was her original Hebrew name, from the word *hadas*, meaning "myrtle." Whether the name Esther was a Persian variant of Hadassah (meaning "star"), used by her to conceal her Jewish ancestry when she entered King Ahasuerus's harem, is unclear. Some commentators believe Esther was also a Hebrew name, but one that sounded more Persian. If it was Hebrew, it was undoubtedly related to *hester*, meaning "hidden," which makes perfect sense considering that she kept her Jewish heritage hidden from the king for at least nine years.

It's much simpler, however, to accept "conventional wisdom" and stipulate that Hadassah was her Hebrew name and Esther was her Persian-into-English name!

The source of the name of Esther's mentor-cousin, Mordecai, is equally problematic. Some commentators suggest that it came from two separate Aramaic words: *mera dachya*, which was a spice that allowed its fragrance to escape only after it had been processed. This sentiment would apply equally well to Mordecai and Esther. On the other hand, some commentators suggest that Mordecai was a Babylonian name, adapted from the god Marduk. Given the care with which most ancient Jews named their children, this derivation seems much less likely.

FEATURES OF THE BOOK ITSELF

In addition to the complete absence of the name of God from its pages, the book of Esther is not mentioned anywhere in the New Testament. Neither was it found among the Dead Sea Scrolls. Likewise, neither the Law nor the sacrificial system is mentioned anywhere in Esther. The same is true of prayer, although we can certainly envision Mordecai and Esther praying.

What Is the Diaspora?

The word *diaspora* comes from an ancient Greek word, meaning "a scattering" or "a sowing of seeds." In general it refers to the dispersion throughout the world of any group of people of similar ethnicity who have been forced to leave their homeland. It has also come to encompass whatever goes on within that group of people, wherever they are—in other words, the diaspora defines where they are but also says something about who they are.

Historically, with respect to the Jews, the word *diaspora* has been used to refer to those Jews (and their descendants) who were exiled from Judea in 586 BC by the Babylonians, and from Jerusalem in AD 135 by the Romans, but were then reestablished in the modern state of Israel in 1948. The same word is now used—probably with even greater frequency—to refer to those Jews, in modern days, who are still living outside of Israel. The first is the historic *diaspora;* the second is the modern *diaspora.*

On the other hand, although most people think of the Jews whenever this word is used, it does not refer exclusively to them in a literal sense. It could also apply to a long list of people groups, down through history, who have been forced to leave their homelands and have then maintained at least a semblance of identity for a definite time period.

The Jews' diaspora, however, is what has ultimately set them apart from all other people groups. Their total diaspora, both historic and modern, has lasted for more than two thousand years, yet they have never lost their ethnic identity. Jews have always been Jews, from biblical times right up to the present day. And those who are now part of the modern diaspora are still recognizable Jews as well—they have not lost their ancient language, traditions, customs, or religion. Contrast this with dozens of other people groups identified in the Bible to see the truth of God's covenant with Abraham—that He would make of Abraham a great nation with members as numerous as the grains of sand on the seashore, and that they would always be His people, set apart for Him by their customs, traditions, and religious observances.

On the other hand, when the wickedness of Haman first seems to be prevailing, Mordecai responds in the traditional Jewish manner, as do many of the other Jews. However, we are told that they respond by fasting but not by praying:

> When Mordecai learned all that had happened, he tore his clothes and put on sackcloth and ashes, and went out into the midst of the city. He cried out with a loud and bitter cry. He went as far as the front of the king's gate, for no one might enter the king's gate clothed with sackcloth. And in every province where the king's command and decree arrived, there was great mourning among the Jews, with fasting, weeping, and wailing; and many lay in sackcloth and ashes. (Esther 4:1–3 NKJV)

WHO, WHEN, WHERE, AND WHY

Although the text itself links its own events to unmistakable dates—and although the author had to have some knowledge of the existence of the Shushan citadel—scholars are still divided as to when (and by whom) the book of Esther was actually written. Some believe it was composed by an unknown author somewhere within the Persian Empire, then carried back to Palestine and added to the books that were eventually accepted as the Old Testament canon. Others believe it more likely that the author of Esther was living in Palestine when he wrote it and that his purpose was to encourage the returning Israelites in their struggle to reestablish the kingdom of Israel after the Babylonian exile by recounting how God had divinely protected many of their brethren in the meantime.

The latter approach would fall under the ancient Hebraic "light-heavy" rules of biblical interpretation. If God could work on His people's behalf under conditions as adverse as what prevailed within the very citadel of their enemies, *how much more dramatically* could He help them in the land of their own destiny? (For a more detailed explanation of the "light-heavy" rules, see the study guide to the book of Romans in this series.)

The book of Esther might also have been used to remind the people of Israel of the eternal covenant that God had established with them back at Mount Sinai after He brought them out of Egypt—and of the obvious fact that no matter how strong and hostile the people who surrounded them might seem to be, God was still in charge and was still able to protect and preserve His own people, wherever they might be. This, despite the corresponding probability that, as foretold in Deuteronomy 11:26–28 (and elsewhere), because of their indifference to God's commandments, they were now under His disciplining curse rather than His blessing.

Many scholars have suggested that either Ezra or Nehemiah wrote the book of Esther. Both had firsthand knowledge of many events in the Persian kingdom regardless of whether they were actually present during Esther's most prominent decade. Also, as leaders of the Jewish people, they both were anxious to do anything they could to provide encouragement and support for what they knew God expected of them. Nothing in the historical record supports either assumption, yet at the same time, nothing argues *against* either one. So we are left to wonder, although it's worth mentioning that we have no need to assume the author was a well-known person.

From a purely historical standpoint, outside sources support many of the background details in Esther. Xerxes (Ahasuerus) was a real king. He ruled the Persians during the time period in question. He also was a legendary drinker, and his behavior toward his own queen, Vashti, as recounted in the first chapter of Esther, certainly accords with what we know of his character. Although the text does not make this clear, many scholars believe Xerxes might have commanded Vashti to appear in the nude, which she quite properly refused to do.

If true, it could even be said that Vashti's sense of propriety, pagan though she might have been, opened the door and ushered Esther onstage, in exactly the right place to do exactly what God knew would eventually be required. Thus we again see evidence, not only of God's overwhelming love for His people, but of His existence "outside the time line" by which we humans insist on connecting all of history together. From that vantage point God is utterly unconstrained by yesterday, today, and tomorrow, for these three concepts mean absolutely nothing to Him.

All of these things are among the lessons we might draw from the book of Esther. They are not of deep doctrinal or theological significance. On the contrary, they are as simple (yet profound!) as only God could make them.

These are My people. I love them. I will protect them. And if that means I have to send a Jewish wife into a foreign household to persuade a Persian king to keep them alive, well . . . let the story begin!

JEWISH VERSUS GREGORIAN CALENDAR

Several events in the book of Esther are keyed to the Jewish calendar, which has remained unchanged since biblical times, and to the Gregorian calendar adopted by most of the rest of the world in AD 1582 after a decree issued by Pope Gregory. The comparisons below show the relationship between the two. The special days in the last column include the seven sacred festivals ordained by God, beginning with Passover (all of which are explained in Leviticus 23). They also include two traditional Jewish holidays: the Feast of Dedication (commonly called Hanukkah) observed by Christ Himself in John 10:22, and Purim, the annual celebration of Esther's role in preserving the Jews, which is what the book of Esther is all about.

Gregorian Calendar	Jewish Calendar	Agricultural Connection	Special Days
March–April	Month 1: Nisan	Latter rains Barley harvest Flax harvest	(1) Nisan 14: Passover *Exodus 12:1–11;* *Leviticus 23:5* (2) Nisan 15–21: Unleavened Bread *Leviticus 23:6–8* (3) Nisan 21: Firstfruits *Leviticus 23:9–14*
April–May	Month 2: Iyyar	Beginning of dry season	
May–June	Month 3: Sivan	Ripening of early figs Vine tending	(4) Sivan 6 (fifty days after Firstfruits): Shavuot (called Pentecost in New Testament) *Leviticus 23:15–22*
June–July	Month 4: Tammuz	Wheat harvest Ripening of first grapes	

July–August	Month 5: Ab	Grape harvest	
August–September	Month 6: Elul	Dates and summer figs	
September–October	Month 7: Tishri	Early rains	(5) Tishri 1: Feast of Trumpets *Leviticus 23:23–25* (6) Tishri 10: Day of Atonement *Leviticus 16; 23:26–32* (7) Tishri 15–21: Feast of Tabernacles *Leviticus 23:33–36*
October–November	Month 8: Marchesvan	Plowing Olive harvest	(8) Kislev 25: Feast of Dedication (Hanukkah) *John 10:22* (Not ordained by God)
November–December	Month 9: Kislev	Grape planting	
December–January	Month 10: Tebeth	Latter rains	
January–February	Month 11: Shebat	Blossoming of almond trees	
February–March	Month 12: Adar	Citrus fruit harvest	(9) Adar 13–14: Purim *Esther 9:26–28* (Not ordained by God)

6 | PROMINENCE

ESTHER 1:1–2:20

Before We Begin . . .

What comes to mind when you think of the book of Esther? What do you think it's really all about? Why do you think God wanted it in the Bible?

If you had to select a hero and a heroine from the book of Esther, before working through this study, who would they be? Why?

ESTHER 1

THE KING DETHRONES QUEEN VASHTI

The book of Esther begins with a mighty feast, lasting almost half a year, given by a powerful earthly king whose name has become almost legendary in secular writings. However, those same extrabiblical historical sources suggest that the feast in question might also have been an extended planning session, during which the king met with the leaders of his army to plan a massive invasion of Greece, which came about during the fourth year of the king's reign. Doubtless the king met with his generals and administrators during the day, then wined and dined them at night.

What was the biblical name of the king who reigned over 127 provinces (v. 1)? Based on the material in the introduction to this study guide, what was his name in most historical texts?

Where was his kingdom (v. 2)? Again, based on the material in the introduction to this study guide, in what modern country would that citadel (or palace) be located if it were still standing?

In what year of his reign did King Ahasuerus make this gigantic feast for all his officials and servants—"the powers of Persia and Media, the nobles, and the princes of the provinces" (v. 3 NKJV)?

How many days did the feast last?

In verse 5 we are told that the same king gave a *second* feast, in which wine was served in golden goblets. We are also given several details about linen, silver, marble, and costly stones, all of which were used in Persia. Even the couches, mentioned in verse 6, were further authenticated by the Greek historian Herodotus. And blue and white, of course, were the Persian royal colors.

WAS THE QUEEN PREGNANT?

It's difficult to be absolutely sure which of Ahasuerus's many queens might have been known in the Bible as Vashti. However, if the queen in question were actually the one known in other historical sources as Amestris, there's at least a small chance that her refusal to appear before the king's guests— fully dressed or not—might have had something to do with her physical condition. In 483 BC, Amestris bore the king a son, Artaxerxes, who succeeded his father in 464 BC. At the time of the banquet, Amestris easily could have been pregnant with little Artie.

For whom was that second feast? In what way do you believe it might have differed from the feast detailed in the preceding verses?

Queen Vashti then sponsored a feast for all the women of the city. But next came the fateful call from the king, who by then was "merry with wine" (v. 10 NKJV).

What order from the king did Queen Vashti refuse to honor (v. 12)? Given what you believe might have been involved in the king's order to display herself before the people, do you think her refusal would have been justified?

What suggestion did the spokesman for the king's wise men, Memucan, give to the king for how to handle Queen Vashti's disobedience (vv. 16–20)?

A TREE BY ANY OTHER NAME

Those who are the tiniest bit familiar with the work of George Frederic Handel, composer of *Messiah* (which is mentioned several times in our study guide to the book of Isaiah because it incorporates so many verses from that book), know that he also composed a number of operas based on biblical characters and stories—sometimes in English, sometimes in Italian, according to the fashion of his day. *Jephtha* (Handel's spelling), *Solomon*, and *Samson* are all good examples of English-language operas. And so, of course, is *Esther.*

Now before you tune this out because it mentions the word *opera* (which, in Italian, combined with *d' musici*, simply means "work of music" and gives us such English words as *operate* and *operation*) please stay with us for just a moment longer! Except for noting that an aria called "Tune Your Harps to Cheerful Strains" is probably the most beautiful piece from all of *Esther* (and begins with an oboe introduction so captivating that some who've sung it have been known to miss their cues!), this is not a dissertation on baroque vocal music.

On the contrary, we wanted to point out that the Bible also provided Handel with *historical* characters whose stories he set to music without any reference to their biblical moorings whatsoever. A case in point comes from the book of Esther, which obviously provided the story for his opera of the same name (and which is one opera that reproduces the original story with relative accuracy).

But as we have pointed out, the king in the book of Esther, known in the Bible as Ahasuerus, is better known in history as Xerxes. And from Handel's opera *Xerxes*, which can only be described as a shallow, secular story about the human failings of that famous Persian general, comes what is probably the best known of all of Handel's compositions, with the possible exception of one or two arias from *Messiah*.

It is commonly known as "Handel's Largo," and it has found its way into just about every hymnal and every compilation of great classical music since the invention of the phonograph more than a century ago. The opera itself was written to an Italian libretto, so the actual "largo" (which, in musical composition, usually means "slow and dignified," which perfectly describes this piece) was called "ombra mai fu." However, this particular melody has also been fitted with words from many different languages, including English. Perhaps the version most familiar to churchgoers would be one called "Love Ye the Lord."

But what was the original all about? Surely a song of such grace and beauty must have been written in praise of a beautiful woman! Well . . . not exactly. In Handel's opera, the largo—whose Italian title means "thy blossoms fair"—is sung by King Xerxes in honor of . . . a plane tree (a tree common to Palestine that sheds its bark) in his garden!

Never mind that the heroine in the story hears Xerxes singing and views the love he expresses for a common tree as an example of an emotional purity so great she cannot help but admire the king himself! Such are the logical vagaries of operatic composition.

What did the king do in response to Memucan's suggestion (v. 22)?

ESTHER 2

ESTHER BECOMES QUEEN

The first few verses of this chapter tell us that King Ahasuerus eventually remembered what Vashti had done and what his advisors had suggested he do in response. It's difficult to tell for certain, but perhaps he needed some time to sober up before he could actually deal with what had happened during that fateful banquet! In any case, by verse 5 events are on the move again, and we are introduced at last to Mordecai and Esther.

What tribe of Israel did Mordecai come from (v. 5)?

What was the blood relationship between Esther and Mordecai? Granted, he treated her as a daughter, but what was their real relationship?

Into whose care were Esther and the other girls placed?

How many maidservants did the king provide Esther to help her with her beauty preparations (v. 9)?

What secret did Mordecai require Esther to keep (v. 10)?

How long was the beauty preparation period (v. 12)?

In verse 15 we are finally told the name of Esther's actual father. What was it?

Verse 16 gives us an interesting insight into the passage of time. It tells us that Esther was called into the king's presence in the seventh year of his reign. Do you remember what year in his reign he held the banquet at which Vashti refused to appear? If you said "the third year," you are correct, which means the replacement process had been going on for about four years when Esther finally got the opportunity God had clearly set up for her.

Verse 17 tells us that Esther would be the new queen, at which point King Ahasuerus made a great feast and proclaimed a holiday in her honor. What was the name of the feast?

PULLING IT ALL TOGETHER . . .

- King Ahasuerus, "who reigned over one hundred and twenty-seven provinces, from India to Ethiopia" (Esther 1:1 NKJV), gave a huge party for the princes and powers under his command.

- This party lasted one hundred and eighty days. It was followed by a separate seven-day party for the local people only, who lived in the capital city, Shushan.

- At the latter party, King Ahasuerus commanded Vashti, his queen, to appear before the people like a trophy, displaying her beauty so that all could see what a terrific choice he'd made.

- Vashti refused, and the king called together his wise men to decide on a proper punishment. They advised him to banish Vashti from his presence and replace her with a new queen.

- The king then sought throughout his kingdom for a new queen. Esther, a beautiful young Jewess, was brought in, along with many other young virgins. She quickly found favor with the eunuchs in charge of the king's harem and received valuable advice (and special favor) from them.

- When Esther finally went in to the king, she was well prepared. Soon she became his favorite, at which point he made her his new queen and threw a large banquet in her honor.

7

NEAR EXTERMINATION

ESTHER 2:21–4:3

Before We Begin ...

The book of Esther contains a surprising development, in which Mordecai rendered a huge service to the king. Without reading ahead, can you explain what he did?

Down through the centuries, in both literature and history, various people in positions of not-quite-enough power have tried to "pull a Haman" and promote themselves into the top spot through various crimes and deceits, including murder. A good example would be Iago from Shakespeare's Othello. Can you name another such villain—real or fictional—from your own memory?

Something happened in Esther 2:21–23 that would have great significance later on. It involved Mordecai and two of the king's eunuchs, but Esther also played an important part. Read the passage below, then answer the questions that follow:

In those days, while Mordecai sat within the king's gate, two of the king's eunuchs, Bigthan and Teresh, doorkeepers, became furious and sought to lay hands on King Ahasuerus. So the matter became known to Mordecai, who told Queen Esther, and Esther informed the king in Mordecai's name. And when an inquiry was made into the matter, it was confirmed, and both were hanged on a gallows; and it was written in the book of the chronicles in the presence of the king. (NKJV)

Who was furious with the king and plotted to kill him?

What did Esther and Mordecai do to save the king's life?

In return, when the whole affair was recorded in the book of the chronicles in the king's presence, whose name was associated with saving the king's life?

If you already know why the above is so important, explain it here:

SACKCLOTH AND ASHES

In addition to Mordecai, the Old Testament speaks of several characters who put on sackcloth and ashes as a sign of repentance, supplication, mourning, and humility. Consider the following:

Repentance

"Therefore I abhor myself, and repent in dust and ashes." (Job 42:6 NKJV)

Supplication

"Then I set my face toward the Lord God to make request by prayer and supplications, with fasting, sackcloth, and ashes." (Dan. 9:3 NKJV)

Humility

So the people of Nineveh believed God, proclaimed a fast, and put on sackcloth, from the greatest to the least of them. Then word came to the king of Nineveh; and he arose from his throne and laid aside his robe, covered himself with sackcloth and sat in ashes. (Jon. 3:5–6 NKJV)

Mourning

O daughter of my people, dress in sackcloth and roll about in ashes! Make mourning as for an only son, most bitter lamentation; for the plunderer will suddenly come upon us. (Jer. 6:26 NKJV)

Jesus Himself also mentioned sackcloth and ashes in this passage from the New Testament:

"Woe to you, Chorazin! Woe to you, Bethsaida! For if the mighty works which were done in you had been done in Tyre and Sidon, they would have repented long ago in sackcloth and ashes." (Matt. 11:21 NKJV)

Ironically, probably because of the association with sack, in modern times we tend to think of sackcloth as a material like burlap—that is, the rough material once used to make sacks for potatoes, onions, and other kinds of produce before the age of plastic netting. But biblical sackcloth (which was, logically enough, also used for sacks) was made of coarse goat hair and was usually black (and would therefore tend to be hot as well, whenever the sun was out), as revealed in this passage near the very end of the Bible:

I looked when He opened the sixth seal, and behold, there was a great earthquake; and the sun became black as sackcloth of hair, and the moon became like blood. (Rev. 6:12 NKJV)

Sackcloth also tended to be rough and scratchy, which is all the more reason for it to be worn as a garment signifying sadness and humility, for it certainly would not be comfortable! In modern times the custom survives in the black armbands that are often worn as signs of mourning.

Ashes represented all the same things, so the sackcloth garment was often rubbed or dusted with ashes. Thus it's easy to see how the symbolism of rubbing a small smudge of ashes on the forehead, as a sign of penitence, eventually evolved into a standard practice within the Catholic church, which continues to celebrate Ash Wednesday every year.

By the eighth century, in the Middle Ages, people who were beyond help and about to die were sometimes laid on the ground on a piece of sackcloth sprinkled with ashes. The priest would then bless the dying person with these words: "Remember that thou art dust and to dust thou shalt return."

ESTHER 3

HAMAN'S CONSPIRACY AGAINST THE JEWS

We are not told why King Ahasuerus promoted Haman in the opening verses of chapter 3. Given what we will soon learn about Haman's character, most likely he achieved his high position through flattery and deceit, but we cannot be sure. What we do know is that through an unholy alliance between Haman and the servants in the king's household, Mordecai and Esther soon found themselves and all their people in mortal danger.

Who was the only person who would not bow down and pay homage to Haman?

When Haman learned that Mordecai would not bow or pay homage, whom did Haman seek to destroy in addition to Mordecai himself? Why do you suppose he went after so many others besides Mordecai?

How did Haman convince the king that all the Jews should be destroyed (v. 8)? What clever (but false) "association" did he establish in the mind of the king?

How much silver did Haman offer to pay to those who fulfilled the king's decree and destroyed all the Jews?

WHY DOES GOD SO OFTEN USE PEOPLE?

The above question is one that most of us probably do not think about very much. We tend to think of God as entirely sovereign—which He is—but we don't always consider *how* He accomplishes His purposes.

Contrary to what many people seem to think, God is not a God of hurricanes and earthquakes, of sudden heart attacks and profound "death's-door" recoveries. Certainly all those agencies are within His command, but ever since He created Adam and Eve, God has demonstrated, over and over, one profound fact likely to be true throughout eternity.

Our God could be a God of isolation. He could do everything entirely on His own, using people as chess pawns and changing the rules whenever He wanted to. But instead, *our God is a God of relationships.* When He created Adam, He made it clear that He desired companionship Himself, and when He created Eve, He made it even clearer that He understood the need for human-to-human companionship as well.

In the story of Esther, God demonstrates once again that He prefers to accomplish His ends by working in partnership with people. Oh sure, he could have sent a crippling disease to shut Haman's mouth before he ever spoke a word against the Jews. He could have wiped out the army Haman had primed and waiting; he could have sent a lightning bolt and burnt down Haman's gallows.

But He didn't. He let Haman's evil run its course, and he countered it decisively with the *opportunity* (and not the *requirement!*) for Esther and Mordecai to step up to the plate and hit home runs. He involved many others as well, beginning with all those who fasted and prayed for Esther before she went in to meet with the king. And, of course, all those Jewish soldiers whose hands He steadied when it came time to fight for their lives.

But as always (think Gideon, Joshua, Jephthah, Deborah, and a host of others we have already mentioned), God used ordinary people to bring about extraordinary circumstances. That sounds almost trite, because you've undoubtedly heard it before—but it's still eternally true.

Should we be any less eager than God to work with others to bring about good results?

On what day was the decree written (v. 12)?

What did the full decree stipulate (v. 13)?

ESTHER 4

ESTHER AGREES TO HELP THE JEWS

What did Mordecai do to express his grief after learning the news? Would this kind of conduct be unusual for any other Jew, given the situation?

How did the rest of the Jews in the land react to the news?

PULLING IT ALL TOGETHER . . .

• Mordecai was sitting near the entrance to the king's palace when he heard two of the king's eunuchs plotting against the king—planning to do him significant harm. Mordecai told Esther, who told the king, who responded by having the plotters hanged and writing down an official version of what had happened.

• For reasons we probably will never know, King Ahasuerus promoted Haman to a high position within his administration. He also commanded all the people to bow to Haman, thus playing into Haman's hands.

• The king's servants watched Mordecai and quickly informed Haman that Mordecai was not paying him the correct homage.

• Haman then convinced the king to have Mordecai hanged for insubordination. But to make matters much worse, he also convinced the king to issue a proclamation authorizing the destruction of all the Jews in the kingdom, for they were all just as disrespectful as Mordecai.

• When Mordecai heard the news, he tore his clothes and put on sackcloth and ashes. Most of the Jews in the city did likewise.

8

CALAMITY AVERTED

ESTHER 4:4–9:19

Before We Begin . . .

In this chapter, Esther will again take her life into her own hands and do something very dangerous. What do you think that will be?

If you already know what will happen to Haman, do you consider it fair? Why or why not?

These five chapters of Esther contain what is certainly one of the greatest turn-arounds in the entire Bible. Think of a Super Bowl team, behind by five, in their own end zone and down to their last timeout. Out of the blue a brand-new quarterback comes in and takes them all the way down the field in seven plays, with three seconds left.

Or think of a presidential election in which the only woman candidate suddenly catches on. She gains one hundred fifty-seven more electoral votes than anyone thought she could and then goes on to eliminate war, poverty, and political friction in the first eighteen days of her new presidency.

The first is probably a little more likely, but hey—we haven't had a female president yet, so we really don't know! More to the point, the Jews of Esther's time undoubtedly thought their situation was even more hopeless than either of the above. Certainly it was a lot more serious. So let's see how it turned out.

In Esther 4:1–5, Esther still didn't know what was going on. So whom did she send to find out what was wrong with Mordecai (v. 5)?

What did Mordecai hope to accomplish by telling Hathach everything (vv. 7–8)?

The next several verses are perhaps the most poignant from all of Esther. They contain one of the best-known quotations in all the Bible, familiar to millions (like those words from Ruth!) whether or not they realize where they came from. Those words, of course, are the ones Mordecai spoke to Esther. Though her response isn't quoted quite so often, it's certainly just as memorable.

Fill in the blanks in the passage below, then answer the questions that follow:

Then Esther spoke to Hathach, and gave him a command for Mordecai: "All the king's _____ and the people of the king's _____ know that any man or woman who goes into the inner court to the king, who has not been called, he has but one law: put all to _____, except the one to whom the king holds out the golden _____, that he may live. Yet I myself have not been called to go in to the king these thirty days." So they told Mordecai Esther's words.

And Mordecai told them to answer Esther: "Do not think in your heart that you will escape in the king's _____ any more than all the other Jews. For if you remain completely _____ at this time, _____ and _____ will arise for the Jews

from another place, but you and your father's house will
_____. *Yet who knows whether you have come to
the kingdom for* _____ _____ _____
_____ _____ *?"*

*Then Esther told them to reply to Mordecai: "Go, gath-
er all the* _____ *who are present in Shushan, and*
_____ *for me; neither eat nor drink for three
days, night or day. My maids and I will fast likewise.
And so I will go to the king, which is against the law;
and* _____ _____ _____ *,*
_____ _____ *!"*

*So Mordecai went his way and did according to all that
Esther commanded him. (Esth. 4:10–17 NKJV)*

How long had it been since Esther had seen the king?

What did Hathach tell Mordecai would happen to Esther if she
were to enter the inner court of the king without being sum-
moned by the king himself?

What was Mordecai's memorable response?

What did Esther ask Mordecai and the other Jews to do for her
(v. 16)?

It's hard to imagine a more tense situation—or one in which the central player displayed more courage. On the other hand, if Mordecai was right and God truly was in charge (and fully able to handle the situation whether or not Esther played her part), maybe it really wasn't all that desperate. At least, not from God's perspective.

Can you think of any way God could have saved the Jews without out Esther's help?

ESTHER 5

ESTHER'S BANQUET

In the events of the next two chapters, we have further evidence of the way that God works on more than one level at once. Note that Esther did not immediately denounce Haman. On the contrary, she let his actions speak for themselves. Let's work through the details.

What did the king do when Esther entered the inner court of his palace?

What did Esther invite the king and Haman to do (v. 4)?

Despite all this, why was Haman upset when he saw Mordecai later on (v. 9)?

Explain in your own words why you think it was so ironic for Haman to boast to his family and friends of his successes (vv. 10–12)? (Note: Irony is defined as "the difference between the truth and what appears to be the truth"!)

Haman's success was soured by what or by whom?

Who was Zeresh?

What did Haman's wife suggest he do before attending the banquet (v. 14)?

ESTHER 6

THE KING HONORS MORDECAI

As before, in the beginning of chapter 6 we have another terrific example of the way God often works. Note that He doesn't swoop down and command the king to realize anything profound or monumental. He simply prepares King Ahasuerus for what's coming by the gentlest, most "internal" of methods.

He also dramatically raises the stakes for Haman! What could be more ironic than turning the tables? What could be a more righteous way to allow Haman to reveal even more of his own evil?

What caused the king to have the book of the records of the chronicles, detailing what Mordecai had done for him, read in the middle of the night?

Once reminded of Mordecai's assistance, the king wanted to honor him. In the ultimate irony, in whom did the king confide to help him decide what honor was appropriate for Mordecai (v. 6)?

At first, whom did this person think the king was planning to honor?

Fill in the blanks in the passage below and see how this person responded to the king's initiative:

And _____ answered the king, "For the man whom the king delights to honor, let a _____ _____ be brought which the king has worn, and a _____ on which the _____ has ridden, which has a royal _____ placed on its head. Then let this _____ and _____ be delivered to the hand of one of the _____ most noble _____, that he may array the man whom the king delights to honor. Then parade him on _____ through the city square, and proclaim before him: 'Thus shall it be done to the _____ whom the king delights to _____!'" (Esth. 6:7–9 NKJV)

Once Haman had the whole story straight, how did he react in private to the king's requirement to honor Mordecai in public (v. 12)?

What was Zeresh's warning to Haman (v. 13)? Was this a wise statement?

ESTHER 7

HAMAN HANGED INSTEAD OF MORDECAI

This chapter begins with the fifth of five banquets recorded in the book of Esther—two given by the king, two given by Esther, and one given by Vashti. It also finesses a fascinating question—that is, how much did Haman know about Esther's ancestry? By working to eliminate the Jews through Mordecai, did he realize that he would also be condemning the king's favorite wife? Or was he aware of where she came from but so utterly convinced of his own cleverness that he thought he could get what he wanted anyway?

In other words, was Haman a victim of his own ignorance or his own arrogance? Write down your answer here before you proceed to the following questions.

Where did the king and Haman go (v. 1)?

The Fast of Esther

The traditional Purim holiday is also preceded by a minor fast, the Fast of Esther, which commemorates the three days Esther and her maidens spent fasting before Esther went in—unbidden—to see the king.

In the modern age, most Jews still hear the book of Esther read aloud during Purim—indeed, hearing it is considered a basic commandment. The book itself is also commonly known as the *Megillah,* meaning "scroll." Actually, four additional books of Jewish Scripture (and Gentile Scripture as well!) are known as megillahs—Ruth, Ecclesiastes, Song of Songs (or Song of Solomon), and Lamentations. But the book of Esther is the one most people mean when they use the expression "the Megillah."

While the book of Esther is being read, it is customary to boo, hiss, stamp your feet, rattle noisemakers, and otherwise make yourself heard whenever Haman's name is heard. The purpose is to "blot out the name" of Haman. Beyond this, the congregants in many Jewish synagogues dress in period costumes and dramatize the book of Esther as they read it, with different people playing the parts of different characters.

Many groups hold carnival-like celebrations on Purim, which may include plays and parodies, Esther look-alike beauty contests, and often hilarious contests to see who can look the most like Mordecai, Haman, and King Ahasuerus. Thus Purim is often referred to as the "Jewish Mardi Gras."

Two more traditions are also generally associated with Purim. The first is to eat, drink, and be merry—and in this unique case, to drink until the person can no longer tell the difference between "Cursed be Haman" and "Blessed be Mordecai." In most congregations this particular tradition is honored more in the breach than in the observance, but it remains a pleasant fantasy all the same!

The second tradition is to send out gifts of food or drink and to make gifts to charity. Also, among many Jews, a common treat at Purim is a triangular, fruit-filled cookie, called *hamentaschen,* German for "Haman's pockets" or, less correctly from a linguistic point of view, "Haman's hats."

What did the king ask Queen Esther on the second day of the banquet?

Summarize Queen Esther's response (vv. 3–4).

Whom did her words reveal as the Jews' adversary and enemy?

The king was obviously angry—so much so that he took a walk in his garden to cool off! But then, to make things even worse, in what compromising position did the king find Haman and his queen when he returned?

What did the king command his servants to do to Haman (v. 10)?

ESTHER 8

ESTHER SAVES THE JEWS

With Haman now among the deceased, things turned even more completely around. First the king assigned new ownership to two important pieces of property.

Whose estate did the king give to Queen Esther (v. 1)?

To whom did the king give his signet ring?

But the story wasn't quite over. Haman was gone, but his evil preparations could have lived on, had Esther not done one more major thing. What was her final plea to the king (vv. 3–6)? Also, given what you already know about the rules of the court, did she literally endanger her life again . . . or not?

As a result, on what day of the year was Haman's decree reversed (vv. 9–14)?

How was Mordecai then treated?

Finally, to complete this chapter, fill in the blanks in the passage below to discover how the Jews (and many of the Persians as well) reacted to all this news.

The Jews had _____ and _____, _____ and _____. And in every province and city, wherever the king's command and decree came, the Jews had _____ and _____, a _____ and a _____. Then many of the people of the land became _____, because fear of the _____ fell upon them. (Esth. 8:16–17 NKJV)

ESTHER 9

THE JEWS DESTROY THEIR TORMENTORS

We now come to the next-to-last chapter of this story, completing the total reversal that began with Haman's death. Haman has been declared a criminal and executed; his power has been transferred to Mordecai; his estate has been given to Esther and assigned to Mordecai to administer. It remains only for his "final triumph" over the Jews to be dramatically reversed.

In what sense does what happened next remind you of what God promised to do to the pagan tribes of Canaan, who opposed the Israelites way back in the book of Exodus? That is, what specific emotion, so decisive here in these concluding verses, did God promise to put into the hearts of the Israelites' opponents if the Israelites would just follow through and do as He commanded?

Who then became prominent in the king's provinces (v. 4)?

What did the Jews do (v. 5)?

What did the Jews not do that set them apart from their would-be tormentors (vv. 5–12)? What were they most interested in preserving and protecting? How does this seldom-acknowledged fact prove it?

In contrast, what do you believe Haman and his people would have done, had they been victorious?

How many of the Jews' tormentors were destroyed in Shushan alone (v. 12)?

How many of the Jews' enemies were destroyed (vv. 12–16)?

On what day after the destruction of their enemies did the Jews institute a feast of celebration? What was it called?

PULLING IT ALL TOGETHER . . .

• As soon as Esther's maids and eunuchs told her why Mordecai was so distressed, she tried to stop him from mourning. When this effort failed, she sent Hathach—equivalent to her chief of staff—to communicate directly with Mordecai.

• Through Hathach, Mordecai told Esther of Haman's evil plan, in all its grisly details. He then told her that she had to do something to save her people.

• When Esther responded by saying that entering into the king's presence without an invitation could mean her death, Mordecai told her she had little choice. At that point Esther agreed to go. These two interchanges inspired two of the Bible's best-known speeches—Mordecai's famous "For such a time as this" speech and Esther's famous "If I perish, I perish" response.

• Esther was received gladly by the king, at which point he promised to grant her any request she might have. Esther then put on two banquets for the king and Haman. At the first, which the Scriptures call a "banquet of wine," she asked them both to come to a second banquet on the next day.

• Haman interpreted all this in his own favor and then had to hold himself back to avoid destroying Mordecai prematurely when he passed him at the city gate. Even so, he began building a gallows for Mordecai in gleeful anticipation of what he thought was coming.

• That night the king had trouble sleeping. So he read from his own kingdom's history the story of how Mordecai had saved his life. Realizing that Mordecai had never been properly rewarded, the next day the king asked Haman (without mentioning Mordecai's name) how Mordecai could be honored.

• Haman presumed that he himself was the intended honoree the king was talking about, so he laid out a lavish plan.

Imagine his anger and chagrin when the king then commanded that he do all these things for Mordecai! But this, of course, only sweetened the taste of Haman's anticipated revenge over Mordecai.

• Esther hosted the king and Haman again the next day. This time, when the king asked what she would like, she told him of Haman's plot to kill all her people and asked the king to spare them—and herself!

• Note that Esther did not specifically ask for revenge, yet revenge came about rather quickly. Thus Haman found himself hanged on his own gallows in front of his own house.

• It remained only for the king to give the Jews his permission to defend themselves against Haman's intended massacre. This they did, killing many of their enemies, after which they established the annual Feast of Purim in celebration of their salvation.

9   Purim and Mordecai

Esther 9:20–10:3

Before We Begin . . .

What do you already know about the Feast of Purim? How and why is it celebrated? By whom?

Where Does the Word *Purim* Come From?

In Esther 3 we are told, "In the first month, which is the month of Nisan, in the twelfth year of King Ahasuerus, they cast Pur (that is, the lot), before Haman to determine the day and the month, until it fell on the twelfth month, which is the month of Adar" (v. 7 NKJV).

The word "they" in the above passage, of course, refers to all the king's servants who had brought Mordecai's refusal to bow to Haman to Haman's direct attention, thus precipitating the kill-all-the-Jews crisis that the book of Esther is all about. This passage tells us that the Hebrew word for "lot" (generally thought of as something similar to dice) was *pur*. Hebrew nouns usually form the plural by adding *im*; for example, Jesus' disciples were known collectively as *talmidim*, while one disciple alone was a *talmid*. Thus we get the word *purim*, meaning more than one lot.

From the same source we also get the word *Purim* in its capitalized version, meaning the holiday the Jewish people have now celebrated for many centuries. By tradition, Purim has become one of the most joyful Jewish holidays of all, commemorating their salvation through the wisdom of Mordecai, the courage of Esther, and the providence of God. Here is a portion of the commemorative text from Esther:

> *So they called these days Purim, after the name Pur. Therefore, because of all the words of this letter, what they had seen concerning this matter, and what had happened to them, the Jews established and imposed it upon themselves*

and their descendants and all who would join them, that without fail they should celebrate these two days every year, according to the written instructions and according to the prescribed time, that these days should be remembered and kept throughout every generation, every family, every province, and every city, that these days of Purim should not fail to be observed among the Jews, and that the memory of them should not perish among their descendants. (Esth. 9:26–28 NKJV)

In accord with the book of Esther, Purim is celebrated on the fourteenth day of the month of Adar, which usually corresponds to March in the Gregorian calendar (see "Jewish versus Gregorian Calendar" in the introduction to this study guide). The thirteenth day of Adar was the day chosen by Haman for the extermination of the Jews, but instead it turned out to be the day on which the Jews battled their enemies for their lives—and won. On the following day the Jews celebrated their survival, which they have continued to do ever since. However, in cities that were walled during the time of Joshua, the Jews celebrate Purim on the fifteenth day of the month, because the book of Esther says that deliverance from the massacre was not complete in Shushan, a walled city, until the following day. Thus the fifteenth is referred to as Shushan Purim.

In leap years, when there are two months of Adar, Purim is celebrated in the second month of Adar. Thus it always occurs one month before Passover. The fourteenth day of the first Adar in a leap year then becomes a minor holiday called Purim Katan, which means "Little Purim." The Jews recognize no specific observances for Purim Katan, but they believe in celebrating the holiday, not mourning or fasting. Some communities also observe a Purim Katan on the anniversary of any day when their community was saved from any other catastrophe, destruction, evil, or oppression.

Among the Jews such days are not hard to find.

The remaining verses of chapter 9 and the entire text of chapter 10 serve as a summary and conclusion of all that went before in the book of Esther. In many respects, this much closing detail is unusual in the Bible, which makes it all the more likely that we need to pay special attention to what God caused to be said.

The Jewish holiday that evolved from the events in Esther was not officially ordained by God, as were the seven holidays He established in Leviticus 23. But surely, just as Christ honored

Hanukkah (i.e., the Feast of Dedication) by going to the temple in Jerusalem to celebrate, Purim has His blessing as well. Whether He agrees with some of the customs that have grown up around it, as detailed elsewhere in this study guide, is another matter—but not central to this discussion.

HOW DID THEY GET THE WORD?

The Scriptures tell us that Mordecai sent letters (more likely they were handwritten copies of the original) to all the Jews under King Ahasuerus's sovereignty, telling what had happened in the city of Shushan. Undoubtedly these were then read aloud to the king's Jewish subjects, just as Paul's letters were read aloud to congregations in Rome, Corinth, Galatia, and other places five or six centuries later. Remember—the printing press hadn't been invented yet, so there's no way each individual could have had his own copy.

And rumor has it that most television stations weren't broadcasting very often in Persia during the sixth century BC.

Purim is a well-established Jewish holiday that more and more Christian congregations are beginning to celebrate as well. It is part of the Judeo-Christian shared heritage, but it's also a story capable of transcending one religion or another, as suggested in this verse: "The Jews established and imposed it upon themselves and their descendants and *all who would join them,* that without fail they should celebrate these two days every year, according to the written instructions and according to the prescribed time" (Esth. 9:27 NKJV, italics added).

Please read through the final verses of Esther and answer the following questions.

Who was officially responsible for making the Feast of Purim an annual celebration (vv. 20–23)?

Why do you think Purim became a required annual custom for all Jews in all generations? A partial answer can be found in verses 24–28, but what is your personal opinion?

ESTHER 10

MORDECAI'S GREATNESS

Esther concludes with one of the Bible's shortest chapters—just ninety-three words in the New King James Version, as reproduced below:

> *And King Ahasuerus imposed tribute on the land and on the islands of the sea. Now all the acts of his power and his might, and the account of the greatness of Mordecai, to which the king advanced him, are they not written in the book of the chronicles of the kings of Media and Persia? For Mordecai the Jew was second to King Ahasuerus, and was great among the Jews and well received by the multitude of his brethren, seeking the good of his people and speaking peace to all his countrymen. (Esth. 10:1–3 NKJV)*

Couldn't have said it better ourselves!

PULLING IT ALL TOGETHER . . .

• Mordecai wrote down all that had happened and sent copies of his letter to all the Jews under the authority of King Ahasuerus, wherever they were.

• He proclaimed the Feast of Purim, to be celebrated annually on the fourteenth and fifteenth days of the month of Adar (see the calendar in the introduction to this study guide).

• The Jews were only too happy to accept Purim and establish it as a revered tradition.

• Queen Esther wrote a similar letter, confirming everything that Mordecai had said.

• Mordecai became justifiably great among the Jews.

COMING TO A CLOSE

S everal anomalies present themselves when we attempt to summarize the book of Esther. For example, the text is absolutely replete with ironic reverses, such as the following:

Esther was a beautiful but unknown girl from what the ruling Persians considered a lower class of citizen. Yet she became the Persian king's favorite and ruled as queen of Persia for at least ten years. She literally risked her life to save her people, for which she received additional honor instead of destruction—again, all within what should have been a Persian Empire at least slightly hostile to a Jewish usurper.

Mordecai was once a hated Jew, yet he was promoted to the top government post by the same Persian king who made Esther his queen. Eventually Mordecai became a great hero to the Jews, and a man to be reckoned with to the Persians.

Haman saw his entire life completely reversed—and ended as well. He went from the highest position in the land, just below the king (compare to Joseph and Pharaoh), to the absolute lowest. The humiliation he intended to inflict on Mordecai was inflicted on him, instead. And the death he was so sure he could bring to Mordecai and his people came knocking at his own door. Not even his ten sons were spared; all were killed and subjected to the additional public humiliation of having their corpses hung as examples for others to see.

In addition to all the above, while the story of Esther is clearly a story of how God protects and provides for His people, nothing in the story suggests that anyone was especially "in tune" with God Himself. So . . . as some commentators and teachers have suggested down through the years, does that mean He will always take care of His people no matter how they behave?

The answer is probably a qualified yes. We know how He took care of them throughout the Bible, and all we have to do is look at the current situation to know that God has been protecting His people throughout most of the last century. He has done the same thing through all the years that came before as well, even though His people have endured some horrific setbacks. The story of Esther and Mordecai is exciting and inspiring, but it is probably no more exhilarating than the story of the founding of the modern nation of Israel in the face of monumental opposition from all over the world.

It's a lot more difficult to find anything positive with respect to the Holocaust. And yet it's not very likely that the Jews would have been allowed to establish Israel as a sovereign nation without that horrible experience behind them. Certainly it was a time of heartbreak and terror, but it also motivated the rest of the civilized world to do something honorable for a change. Granted, the let's-be-fair-to-the-Jews mood didn't last very long, but God achieved His obvious purpose in spite of the fickleness of other nations.

What's the point of all this rambling? How do we tie it into the story of Esther? Well, ever since George Santayana spoke his immortal words, we all claim to know that "those who cannot learn from history are doomed to repeat it." Thus millions of people, here in the modern age, really do recognize that God always protects His people. Therefore they will never bet against them. But millions or even *billions* more, especially in the Middle East, have not learned that lesson and continue trying to annihilate the Jews every single day.

Humankind never seems to run out of hatred for God's people, but rest assured that God will never run out of Esthers either.

HOW TO BUILD YOUR REFERENCE LIBRARY

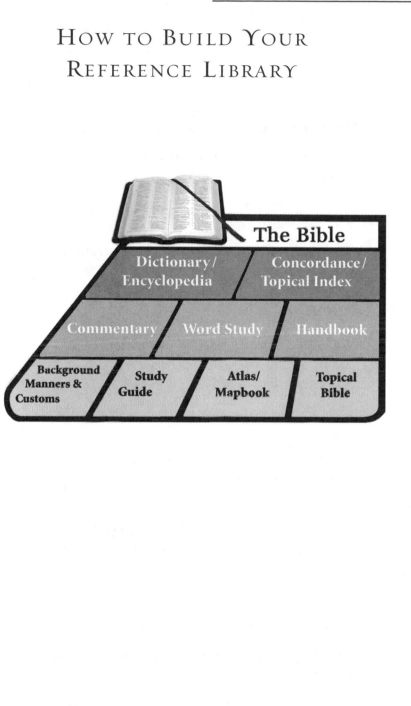

GREAT RESOURCES FOR BUILDING YOUR REFERENCE LIBRARY

DICTIONARIES AND ENCYCLOPEDIAS

All About the Bible: The Ultimate A-to-Z® Illustrated Guide to the Key People, Places, and Things

Every Man in the Bible by Larry Richards

Every Woman in the Bible by Larry Richards and Sue Richards

Nelson's Compact Bible Dictionary

Nelson's Illustrated Encyclopedia of the Bible

Nelson's New Illustrated Bible Dictionary

Nelson's Student Bible Dictionary

So That's What It Means! The Ultimate A-to-Z Resource by Don Campbell, Wendell Johnston, John Walvoord, and John Witmer

Vine's Complete Expository Dictionary of Old and New Testament Words by W. E. Vine and Merrill F. Unger

CONCORDANCES AND TOPICAL INDEXES

Nelson's Quick Reference Bible Concordance by Ronald F. Youngblood

The New Strong's Exhaustive Concordance of the Bible by James Strong

COMMENTARIES

Believer's Bible Commentary by William MacDonald

Matthew Henry's Concise Commentary on the Whole Bible by Matthew Henry

The MacArthur Bible Commentary by John MacArthur

Nelson's New Illustrated Bible Commentary

Thru the Bible series by J. Vernon McGee

HANDBOOKS

Nelson's Compact Bible Handbook

Nelson's Complete Book of Bible Maps and Charts

Nelson's Illustrated Bible Handbook

Nelson's New Illustrated Bible Manners and Customs by Howard F. Vos

With the Word: The Chapter-by-Chapter Bible Handbook by Warren W. Wiersbe

For more great resources, please visit *www.thomasnelson.com.*

NELSON IMPACT™ STUDY GUIDES

NELSON IMPACT
A Division of Thomas Nelson Publishers
Since 1798
www.thomasnelson.com

To find these and other inspirational products visit your local Christian retailer
and www.nelsonimpact.com

The Finest Study Bible EVER!

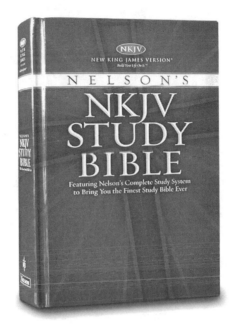

Nelson's NKJV Study Bible helps you understand, apply and grow in a life-long journey through God's Word.

NKJV
NEW KING JAMES VERSION®
Build Your Life On It.™

NELSON IMPACT
A Division of Thomas Nelson Publishers
Since 1798

The Nelson Impact Team is here to answer your questions
and suggestions as to how we can create more resources
that benefit you, your family, and your community.

Contact us at Impact@thomasnelson.com